Frugality & Your Retirement Lifestyle: Live Your Dreams

Published by BookLocker.com, Inc., Bradenton, FL.

Printed in the United States of America on acid-free paper.

BookLocker.com, Inc.
2012

First Edition

Frugality & Your Retirement Lifestyle: Live Your Dreams

Jeffrey Webber

DISCLAIMER

This book details the author's personal experiences with and opinions about frugality and retirement. The author is not licensed financial consultant.

The author and publisher are providing this book and its contents on an "as is" basis and make no representations or warranties of any kind with respect to this book or its contents. The author and publisher disclaim all such representations and warranties, including for example warranties of merchantability and financial advice for a particular purpose. In addition, the author and publisher do not represent or warrant that the information accessible via this book is accurate, complete or current.

The statements made about products and services have not been evaluated by the U.S. government. Please consult with your own Certified Public Accountant or financial services professional regarding the suggestions and recommendations made in this book.

Except as specifically stated in this book, neither the author or publisher, nor any authors, contributors, or other representatives will be liable for damages arising out of or in connection with the use of this book. This is a comprehensive limitation of liability that applies to all damages of any kind, including (without limitation) compensatory; direct, indirect or consequential damages; loss of data, income or profit; loss of or damage to property and claims of third parties.

Please understand that this book is not intended as a substitute for consultation with a licensed financial professional. Before you begin any financial program, or change your lifestyle in any way, you will consult a licensed financial professional to ensure that you are doing what's best for your financial condition.

This book provides content related to topics finances and economic living. As such, use of this book implies your acceptance of this disclaimer.

Contents

INTRODUCTION

A most important consideration during your retirement years is having enough financial resources to meet your needs. The dilemma here is being clever enough to be able to predict those needs.

As we are living longer, healthier lives, we do indeed have the time to rediscover, redefine, and reinvent ourselves. I really do believe that we should create a revitalized outlook for the future. Part of the planning process here is an attempt to pursue our passions and interests.

As I've indicated in my previous books, an absolutely necessary step is the creation of a plan for retirement that you will definitely follow. At the time of this writing, I've been retired for eleven years. I retired from teaching at the age of 55. In an effort to formulate that plan, my wife and I have led a very active lifestyle and experimented with a variety of activities to devise a solid and realistic plan.

When you have come up with a plan, you want to see if your projected income and savings can meet the expenses associated with the associated goals.

Allyn Freeman and Robert Gorman, authors of *Reworking Retirement,* suggest that you consider the following sources of retirement income in an effort figure out your earning potential. Needless to say, income from these sources will help you prepare to implement your plan and how frugal you may have to be.

- savings – money in savings, money markets, and IRA accounts
- pensions – employer-defined plans
- Social Security payments – if you are eligible

- employer-defined plans – including 401(k) and 403(b) plans, where the employee invested pre-tax funds that were matched by the employer
- work – if you are still working

It is important that you consider ideas in your plan that include things that you really want to do. That would involve activities that you've always wanted to do now and in the past. Start simply. Work out a retirement schedule that will not overburden you. You ultimately want to feel a deep sense of satisfaction.

Given the nature of our fluctuating economy, you may even have the desire or need to continue working part-time. Again, there is nothing wrong with that. Working during retirement can readily be considered part of the aforementioned reinvention process. Many people enjoy working too much to give it up. You can also view work as a means to achieve and end. That is, if you've designed those retirement goals working can help with funding.

CHAPTER 1: WHAT IS A FRUGAL RETIREMENT?

It is significant you understand from the outset that this is not a book about how to be cheap during your retirement years.

I would like you, the reader, to come away with a feeling of satisfaction from rediscovering yourself. That is, try to live a creative, innovative, and fun lifestyle that is within your means financially. Frugal living during retirement does not need to entail obstacles to living your dreams. You may not need to change your whole lifestyle. It is all a matter of how you approach frugality.

Being frugal involves getting a better deal and may lead to you having fun and doing the things you want for a longer period of time. You may need to evaluate your lifestyle and adjust your expenses in an effort to allow you to do more and different things that are important sources of enjoyment during these years. Certainly your income must satisfy your expense needs. Changing an existing lifestyle during retirement may simply only involve reorganization. Basically speaking, a frugal retirement is carefully planned. You spend your money wisely to gain the maximum benefits. Ultimately, you would like to have a lot of fun with only minor adjustments. In fact, with a little creativity, you may need less retirement income. And, you may not need to incur ongoing debt with that credit card. If you intend to base your retirement strictly on leisure activities, the amount of money you spend could be excessive.

If you are concerned about the amount of money you will have available to live your desired retirement lifestyle, it is important that you create some sort of monthly budget. When that process is complete you will know how much you have available, where you may be able to cut back, and plan ahead for future expenses. Indeed, this plan will help keep you out of debt. You can begin the process by simply getting a pad, drawing a line down the center labeling one side "income" and the other "expenses." After writing everything down, including that pack of gum, you may be amazed at the amount of money you are wasting.

As you develop your retirement plan, consider how important personal development and enrichment and productivity are in addition to leisure. In terms of learning, the cost can be pretty reasonable. You will find that public universities and community colleges often provide courses at nominal cost for seniors and retirees. Courses may be offered at your local senior citizen center or park and recreation department. Nonprofit organizations such as Elderhostel (*roadscholar.org*) sponsor low-cost educational travel opportunities around the world. Obviously, you can explore individual hobbies or activities. Productivity activities can even be a better bargain, especially if you consider volunteering. As a volunteer you can give back and perhaps engage in a learning experience with little or no cost to you.

I suggest that you begin by evaluating your expenses, both current and anticipated. Prioritize items in your budget related to enjoying your retirement. Focus on areas that may seem a bit too indulgent or excessive. Sometimes we can take for granted our luxury cars (and associated taxes) when a more down-to-earth vehicle will do. Consider items in your budget that are most important to your enjoying retirement. Perhaps you will need to make lifestyle adjustments that reduce expenses. The end result may free up a bit of money that can be used for other things. Ultimately, these actions may readily reduce debt and lead you down a path to enjoyable retirement lifestyle. Try to stick with your lifestyle commitments. Living a frugal retirement lifestyle may involve some experimentation.

Erin Botsford, in her book, *The Big Retirement Risk,* feels that your net worth may not be relevant to your retirement lifestyle, unless it is in a form that can be easily converted to cash to assist with your expenditures. So, if you are an art collector and you add the value of the art to your net worth, it may not necessarily support your lifestyle unless you have buyers ready. Then it becomes an income-producing vehicle.

Frugal Retirement Living (*frugal-retirement-living.com*) suggests some retirement options for you that you may have never before considered:

- live aboard a sailboat
- live in an RV
- live overseas
- small space living
- relocation

They suggest that the above options do not represent cheap living. Rather, they are examples of ways to live frugally.

Relocation may be something for you to think about if you would like to enjoy retirement in a most frugal fashion. There are lists of frugal states, countries, and even retirement communities available, which suggest ideal retirement locations. Please refer to the chapter in this book on "Frugal Relocation."

Another possibility that I can highly recommend is obtaining another residence in the form of a condominium. We own a condo in a beautiful over-55 community in a small town in Arizona. Our neighbors are very friendly and we do, indeed, help each other when the occasion arises. Our location is central to everything. Central living does have advantages. We can walk or bike to the library, community center, shopping, doctors, and the center of town. There are a number of restaurants as well as a new movie theatre complex and a community theatre nearby that we can walk to for entertainment. This obviously reduces transportation costs as well as time spent traveling. In addition, we are healthier because we are more physically active. Potential medical costs may be reduced as a result. As you know, property prices are quite reasonable these days. The condo concept is great because for the most part, no maintenance is required and I worry less about the property when I am away.

Living aboard a sailboat can be very reasonable, especially since you save on utilities (wind and solar generators).

Small space living can simply be a matter of downsizing. Many of us wander around a large home that we really do not need. Unfortunately, making such a move can be difficult for some of us because we may be forced to dispose of possessions that we've accumulated over al lifetime.

My wife and I have been RVers for forty-two years. I can tell you with first hand experience, this is a great way of life. And, with the available variety of RVs for purchase, there is something for everyone. I will discuss more about the frugal nature of the RV lifestyle in a later chapter. For the most detail, I recommend that you read my last book, *RVing & Your Retirement Lifestyle.*

Utilizing Online Retirement Calculators

There are a variety of on online calculators available to assist you. For example, *cnn.money.com* offers links to help you to "run your numbers." Additionally, you can simply type in "retirement calculator" into your favorite search engine and come up with a lengthy list of programs.

The calculators below are generally easy to use.

- FINRA (*finra.org*) – The Financial Industry Regulatory Authority is an independent organization that oversees brokerage firms. This tool is straightforward and simple to use.
- AARP (*aarp.org*) – The American Association of Retired Persons features a calculator that offers the ability to combine information from two people and change your rates of return over time.
- T. Rowe Price (*troweprice.com*) offers an easy-to-use calculator called a Retirement Planning Worksheet.

Control Your Debt

Ideally, we would all like to have a handle on our credit card debt as well as other payments in an effort to really enjoy our retirement to the fullest. Unfortunately, if you've entered retirement burdened with these financial obligations, your leisure lifestyle may become more of a challenge.

The authors of *Retire Happy* suggest the following:

1. If you have large credit card balances, try to transfer that balance to a new card with a lower interest rate without an associated fee.
2. Do pay off balances with a system. Create a payment system and definitely stick to it.
3. Do not take out a home equity loan to pay off your debt unless you can definitely repay the loan within about two years. Obviously, you do not want to risk losing your home. And, you do not want to end up paying more interest than if you kept your high-interest credit card.
4. Do not take any money from a retirement plan to pay off your debt.

5. Think about switching to a debit card. As you probably know, the amounts of any purchases are immediately deducted from your account.
6. Minimize your future use of your credit cards. Certainly that would include any unwise impulse buying.

Follow the 4 Percent Rule

Do you recall what I said earlier in this book regarding the nature of enjoying a frugal retirement? This text does not advocate living a cheap lifestyle. Rather, it is about making the most of your assets.

Consumer Reports Magazine suggests that many financial advisors encourage you follow the 4 percent rule. Withdrawing 4 percent annually has been shown to preserve your capital for at least 30 years in even strained economic environments, assuming that you rebalance your portfolio regularly.

They talk about new mutual funds called managed-payout or income-replacement funds that attempt to provide investors with a regular payout while leaving rebalancing to a fund manager. I do not intend to discuss at length financial strategies in this book. However, if you do indeed have a trustworthy financial manager, these funds may be worth examining. Remember, you want your assets to last as long as possible.

CHAPTER 2: THE INTERNET & YOUR FRUGAL RETIREMENT

In my years spent as a technology facilitator for a school district, I soon came to realize that the Internet does indeed put the world at your fingertips. And, this is especially significant for those of us entering our "Third Age". To reiterate, that is the period of time after family and work.

We can now accomplish many of the tasks that we heretofore had to use our automobile to complete. Additionally, we can reduce our use of snail mail. The Internet allows us to take on many of our tasks in a more frugal fashion, saving gas and postage. I do most of my shopping and payment of bills online.

In my second book, *Technology & Your Retirement Lifestyle: Tools For the New You,* I discuss in detail the functional day-to-day uses of technology for the retiree.

In this chapter, I'd like to discuss some of the ways being online can be a frugal move and fit in with that all important plan for retirement.

The chapter in this book on Frugal Travel Ideas will discuss in detail ways the Internet can save you money on your travel plans.

Getting Online Frugally

Before going online to save money, let us discuss some suggestions for saving money getting online.

I should note here that at the time of this writing, most of the Internet companies were offering very reasonable specials in an effort to gain your business. By all means, visit *att.com, verizon.com*, and *comcast.com*.

If you are already connected and are upset about the cost of your high-speed Internet, contact your Internet service provider and attempt to negotiate a better price. This process becomes more effective if you can play one provider against the other and make them compete for your business. If you go to a website such as *whitefence.com* you can readily obtain quotes and then have a basis to negotiate.

You may be connected with the provider's customer retention department. These days they will most likely to whatever it takes. At our Arizona home I have been very successful in this endeavor with our provider in gaining renewals of three-month introductory specials. Further, package deals frequently change, depending on the services that you need.

The Magic Word: App

Is there anyone these days that does not know what an app is? In case you are one of the few, an app is computer software that is designed to perform specific tasks—and the tasks are many. You can do things like edit photos, listen to music, and even comparison shop. They can be used through your 3G network or through wi-fi. There are many apps out there. A recent count from the Apple App Store suggests that they alone offer over 500,000 apps. These days they are most readily used on your mobile device. Many apps are free while others may cost as little as $1.99.

Since we talking about frugality, there are many money-saving apps out there. Some examples include:

- finding the lowest gas prices
- diagnosing and estimating costs of repairs and service on your car

- deals for dining out
- supermarket comparison calculators
- shopping apps that scan barcodes to give you info on the lowest prices of an item online and in stores, including groceries with associated coupons
- bank mobile apps that allow you to pay bills (while saving the cost of stamps), and even make bank deposits by snapping photos of the check (which allows you to save gas)
- travel apps for airfare, hotels and cars

Volunteering: Do it Virtually (& Frugally)

I feel very strongly about giving back. In fact, that was the subject of my last book, *Volunteering & Your Retirement Lifestyle.*

If you would like volunteering to be part of your retirement plan, part of the process of reinventing yourself during this period, you can do so frugally. You do not even have to leave the comfort of your home or RV. The process is call virtual volunteering. You can volunteer without being present.

Examples of online volunteering include mentoring (helping students with homework responsibilities or job skill development), and tele-tutoring.

If you have technical expertise, you may be able to conduct online research where you are asked to gather information on a program or legislation. Another example would be to update information on a database. There may also be a need for advocacy that would involve posting information to online communities. You may be able to volunteer management assistance, proofread, or even design websites. See the chapter in this book on frugal hobby suggestions for more information on virtual volunteering.

Organizations to assist you with virtual volunteering include VolunteerMatch (*volunteermatch.org*). They service around 40,000 organizations. Their database of openings is very easy to search.

Then there is Elder Wisdom Circle (*elderwisdomcircle.org),* which is a nonprofit association of elders who offers advice to young people.

Serviceleader.org has a very informative link at their website to assist you in preparing for an location virtual volunteering opportunities.

I highly recommend that you download the free Virtual Volunteering Guidebook (*serviceleader.org/virtual/guidebook*). It fully explains every aspect of virtual volunteering.

Keep in Touch With Your Family Frugally

Given the nature of our busy lives and the distances that can separate us from our family members, the Internet has made the "global village" much smaller. We can keep in touch with less expense and certainly less travel. I communicate with family members worldwide through a variety of mechanisms.

In today's world, one of the most convenient ways to stay in touch is email. Most people have some Internet access available either privately or publicly. And, email can be done through a variety of mobile devices.

Another very common way to keep in touch online is through instant messaging. If all parties have the capacity, you can utilize a webcam and videoconference. We do this constantly to keep in touch with our granddaughter. Skype (*skype.com*) is the software that we use regularly, and it is free.

You can also take advantage of online photo albums in an effort to keep up with the latest happenings and activities.

There is also the option of starting a blog. Posting messages to a blog can serve as an online journal. Twitter has become popular due to its simplicity and ease of use.

Oftentimes, blogs are incorporated into social networking sites such as MySpace and Facebook. These sites provide a fun way to keep in touch with distant family. Users post notes, pictures, and videos, and update their daily status and even play interactive games.

Virtual Tours

In case you are not familiar with the terminology "virtual tour", it is basically a computer (or other device) presentation of a real place so as to give the effect of actually being there. You are viewing what can be a panoramic image of a location and you feel the sensation of moving through the represented space. In another words, you are traveling to another location in the comfort of your computer or mobile device. This is a frugal way to experience new locations as well as a helpful tool in the planning stages for an actual trip.

Here are some examples:
- *whitehouse.gov* – Whitehouse tours
- *elvis.com/graceland* – a close-up tour of Elvis' home
- *egyptvoyager.com* – virtual tours of Egypt
- *virtualfreesites.com* – tour collections of museums and exhibits

Shopping Online

In case you do not know what shopping online is, it is the process whereby consumers directly buy goods and services from sellers over the Internet. For specific suggestions see the chapter in this book on Frugal Shopping Tips.

CHAPTER 3: FRUGAL SHOPPING TIPS

As you can surmise by now, I have a thing about getting the most for my dollar. I put a great deal of effort into not paying more than I have to. Again, this is not being cheap. It is a strategy that promotes the idea of doing the best with the assets that I have available. That philosophy applies to all of my daily living activities.

For most of us, developing frugal shopping skills can be a simple process. It basically comes down to a process of exploring the various alternatives available to you that allow you to best utilize your financial resources. The following paragraphs offer some useful suggestions for shopping for goods other than groceries.

General Suggestions

The following strategies will ultimately save you money:

If you can, avoid the middleman when you shop. Of course, this process becomes easier if you shop online. And, you can compare online prices with those in stores.

Try to control impulse buying. Ask yourself whether you really need the item in question.

Buy in bulk if it will save you money. Stockpiling items on sale will also add savings.

Shop at thrift or consignment stores. We've made some incredible deals on good quality furniture over the years. Remember, there are stores that sell varying levels of quality.

Check out the clearance racks at the store.

Be certain to check prices in the warehouse clubs. It is important to compare prices of big-ticket items to be sure you are getting the best deal. As I've mentioned previously, if you have a smartphone, it could be of great service to you.

Download the RedLaser app, which will allow you to compare prices on the spot. You will find more information on food shopping at these clubs in the chapter on Staying Healthy in this book. Here are some suggestions on ways to save at these clubs presented by the website, Financially Fit (Yahoo Finance):

- Stick to one membership. Otherwise, you could end up spending more than $100 just to get inside the stores.
- Perhaps you do not need to buy a membership at all. Often warehouse clubs allow a member to bring along one guest. You could also consider splitting the cost of a membership with a family member.
- Compare prices with other retailers.
- Buy the store brand. Many of the clubs carry their own brands of cleaning products, detergent, and pet food.
- Make use of store perks and discount offers. That would include gas stations, car-care centers, and cafeterias.
- Do not plan too far ahead particularly when it comes to food. You may end up having to store items for months at a time.

Consumers Reports offers the following suggestions and I agree whole-heartedly with all of them.

1. Do not simply accept the asking price for big-ticket items—you can haggle. I have had great success with such things as free delivery, elimination drop-off charges for rental cars, and airline fares when I call the airline directly.
2. Offer to pay cash for an item in exchange for a discount.
3. Say no to extended warranties. Products may easily outlast those expensive additions without the charges.

4. Consider refurbished models when buying electronics. Be certain that they have a valid warranty and that you deal with reliable vendors. I have found that buying floor models can be a great frugal approach.

Do not forget that you can save substantial money on open-box items. Sometimes buyers return merchandise because of the color being wrong, or it may simple be a decision change. I recently purchased a new TV from Target. The box had only been opened and then sealed closed again. The sale price was one-half of the original price, and the item was not even removed from the package. Be certain that you thoroughly check and compare prices for new merchandise with potential manufacturers rebates. Rebate amounts can at time be substantial. In addition, be sure to check return policies.

When purchasing big-ticket items, as I previously discussed, do not hesitate to attempt to negotiate a better price by speaking directly with a floor manager. You could save an additional 15%. And, it is always good to come in with a comparison price that will give you better ground to stand on. If you have a smartphone or iPad, by all means download the aforementioned RedLaser app.

Jeff Yeager, author of *The Cheapskate Next Door*, offers some additional suggestion when considering big-ticket purchases:
1. Always be friendly and polite when asking for a discount.
2. Be honest, but don't be shy. Express your concerns about the quality of a product. That may get you a discount.

3. Watch for competitor's sale prices. Prices can readily be matched.
4. Let the salesman name a price first. Otherwise, you could sell yourself short.
5. Avoid negotiating early in the week. I feel that better deals are made on Fridays or Saturdays.
6. Inquire about discounts for AARP or AAA members.

Outlet Shopping

If you like to shop at outlet centers, Consumer Reports recommends the following ways to shop and save:

- Before you begin your shopping expedition, check the outlet center website to see store locations so you can park and shop strategically.
- Shop early in the day when crowds are smaller and merchandise has not been picked over.
- Look for off-season goods.
- Join shopper programs for exclusive promotions and programs and coupons. Sign up for email alerts.
- Seek other discounts. Some centers offer deals for seniors and the military. Go to the center's website for details.
- Know the return policy.
- You may want to go the center's management office to check for unadvertised sales.
- Many outlet center goods are designed to sell for less than retail goods, so do not assume they are exact copies. Often, items may not be the same quality as retail stores. However, that does not assume that the quality of outlet center goods is inferior.

Dollar Stores and Secondhand Stores

I know a great many people (including my family) that regularly patronize the dollar stores. That is a frugal way to stock up on household goods. Stuff like gift-wrap, bags, notebooks, paper plates, envelops and napkins can be a deal. However, if you are looking at merchandise with expiration dates, be certain to check those dates.

Secondhand stores such as Goodwill and the Salvation Army offer deals on gently-used clothing that can be quite good. Look for even better deals on senior citizen discount days or monthly Saturday discounts of 50%

Frugal Yard Sale Suggestions

My wife has been a fan of yard sales for as long as I can remember. Over the years she as really found some outstanding deals. In order to find these deals, you need to know where and how to look.

Money Magazine offers the following suggestions:

1. Focus on moving sales or older homes. For practical goods, moving sales are better than run-of-the mill garage sales since people may be unloading goods that are in better condition.
2. Know your sizes. You do not want to get home and find the item you bought does not fit.
3. Think about frames when looking at art. They can be worth quite a bit.
4. Test the electronics to be certain that they work.
5. Look carefully at costume jewelry.
6. Heavy items can be cheaper at yard sales, especially when you pick up the item.
7. Be careful with mattresses and upholstered furniture; the risk of bedbugs can be high.

Specific Online Suggestions

I have to admit that I am a self-proclaimed fanatic about shopping online. There is very little (with the exception of groceries) that I do not purchase online, but you can even buy groceries online if you like to stockpile. The following are some money-saving strategies that will help you keep in line with that all-important frugal approach during retirement.

Consumers find a product by visiting a website of the retailer directly or as the result of a search using a shopping search engine. Payment is made most commonly by check, debit card, credit card, or even money orders. The delivery of an item can be made by downloading (if possible), in-store pickup, or shipping. Retailers like Target and Walmart often provide free shipping directly to their stores.

If you are shopping for furniture, remember that more than half of the furniture sold in the U.S. is made in North Carolina. You can save 40% to 50% off regular prices. Check out *highpointfurniture.com* for examples of deals.

I recommend that you begin your shopping by doing a simple Google search for the specific items. Specifically, try Google Shopping (*www.google.com/shopping*) or *shopping.com*. Those sites will offer you general price comparisons. One of the key things you will want to look for is free shipping and when possible, no sales tax. These days you will find most anything you need through *Amazon.com* and its vendors. You can get even lower prices with the help of promotional codes for Amazon or at the Amazon Warehouse, which features more heavily-discounted open-box items or items that have been returned that are guaranteed.

If you are looking for products reviews, check out a website such as *buzzillions.com*. There you will find basic customer reviews, which may assist you in deciding which products to avoid.

Amazon offers Amazon Prime for for an annual fee of $79, which provides you with free two-day shipping on a huge variety of items, plus a number of additional benefits. I've saved a great deal of money with this because you do not need to order the $25 minimum to qualify for free shipping and you do not need to wait a longer time for your orders.

MSN Money (*moneycentral.msn.com*) recommends some sites for the top online shopping deals:

- *overstock.com* – This is their reigning champ of bargain sites due to its breadth of merchandise and great prices. They specialize in excess merchandise from other retailers.
- *shopzilla.com* – This site has been a longtime leader in including user ratings and feedback to bring to the surface great deals.
- *pricegrabber.com* – Offers great deals and great product information with lots of reviews.

I would certainly add *bizrate.com* and *nextag.com* to that list because they do indeed offer a large product base. In addition, sites like DealTime, MySimon, PriceGrabber, and *shopping.com* will also save you time and money. Many of the above sites will even send you an alert when the price of a specific item drops. Don't forget to figure in the cost of shipping. If you check around, you may even find that some of these super-discounted daily deal sites ship free.

For deals on electronics, go to sites such as *tigerdirect.com* or *newegg.com*. These sites maintain a good record of reliability, as well as low prices. I have done business with both and have had no problems.

If you are a member of AARP (and everyone our age should be), be certain to visit their link (*discounts.aarp.org*) on discounts. There you will find discounts galore including dining and entertainment, home, auto and technology, and health and wellness. Their limited time offers involve car rentals, cruises, and travel opportunities (from AARP Travel). You will also find hundreds of grocery coupons. If you register at the site, you can even customize your shopping preferences so you can view what is most relevant to your needs. They will also email you alerts for the limited-time offers. Throughout this book, I have been espousing the benefits of belonging to AARP. These discount offers are simply add to the list.

WikiHow (*wikihow.com*) has some ideas about how to save money shopping online:

1. Use sites that will offer you money back in the future such as "ebates."
2. Try searching for the product you are looking for on comparison sites such as *shopping.com*. This process can save time.
3. Always check eBay for the products that you are looking for as you can often find great deals on new and mint-condition merchandise. Be certain to read associated customer reviews.
4. Try ordering catalogs from *catalogs.com* as they sometimes offer exclusive offers that can be used online.
5. If an online retailer has a store near you, you may want to consider stopping by for the following reason. If you want something that is not in stock in the store, you can often order it from the website with free shipping.

GROUP BUYING WEBSITES

Are you a "coupon clicker"? These days many consumers enjoy the thrill of seeking out deep discounts. Group buying websites offer deep discounts that change daily. There is much appeal attached to those sites including great prices and values. That approach encourages many people to return to the site each day. One of the biggest sites is *groupon.com*. Currently there are 50 million subscribers in 37 countries.

One of the main advantages of these sites is the discovery of new businesses in the local area. People want to find out about these businesses.

Here are a few tips for using daily-deal sites:
- Set up a separate e-mail account so you can go through these deals quickly.
- Not all deals are bargains. Be certain to comparison shop.
- Be sure you know the deal's expiration date.
- Read the fine print.

Other examples of group buying websites include:
1. *buywithme.com*
2. *yipit.com*
3. *blackboardeats.com*

GETTING THE LOWEST PRICE

There are some sites that assist you in getting the lowest price on almost anything.

If you would like to book a cruise and save big by booking last minute, check out *lastminutecruises.com* and *vacationstogo.com*.

Would you like to compare gas prices in your area, log onto *gasbuddy.com* or *fuelmeup.com* to get an idea.

Be certain to look for customer reviews of other companies. You may also find that websites of major companies such as Costco, Walmart, and Target offer better prices than the retail establishments themselves. In addition, if an online retailer has a store near you and the item is not in stock at the store, you can often order the item from their website with free shipping. Sears even allows customers to order from their website with no shipping charges.

If you are searching for electronic products, readers of Consumer Reports magazine rated electronic stores by price, service and product quality. The highest-rated online stores were *crutchfield.com, BHphotoVideo.com*, and *amazon.com*. For walk-in stores, independent stores, Costco, and the Apple stores were the winners. The consensus is that readers seem to prefer online shopping online because of price considerations and convenience.

Then there are the increasingly popular coupon sites where you would print out coupons. Those sites include *groupon.com, dealchicken.com, CouponChief.com, RetailMeNot.com,* and many more.

By all means visit the "deal of the day" sites such as *dealchicken.com* for daily specials. My wife and I recently acquired a great deal on ballroom dance lessons from a local studio. We purchased a series of private lessons for 50% off the regular price. There are also Groupon and LivingSocial that offer discounts on goods and local services. Kohl's, Target, Meijer, and Sears also offer daily deals on their websites. Google has joined in with Google Offers. The most important consideration here is trying not to spend money on things you would not buy normally if you were monitoring your expenses. Actually, this is a fun way to spend.

Log onto Facebook and Twitter for deals at your favorite sites. There are a great many retailers that post exclusive deals, sales, and coupon codes. You can check the site's homepage to see if they are linked to Facebook or Twitter.

Catalogs.com sometimes presents exclusive offers that can be used online as well as customer ID numbers that allow companies to offer you discounts.

Frugal Credit Card Use

There are definite strategies to consider when you are shopping with your credit card.

From the time you make your purchases until the payment is due is usually around 30 days. In essence, you are using the credit card company's money for free during that time.

I never use cash for any major shopping. I pay off my balance in full each month to avoid any interest charges. In addition, I use a card with no annual charge that offers airline points or cash back.

In an effort to avoid complications with identity theft, I suggest that you carry one or two credit cards at most. You might also consider carrying one debit card as well, which could help you ease the burden of potential credit debt.

The following additional suggestions offer you some basic rules for credit card use:

- Pay your bill on time in an effort to avoid interest charges.
- Charge only what you are certain you can pay off each month.
- Use credit card incentives wisely, especially if you fly frequently.

CHAPTER 4: HOBBIES AND NEWFOUND PASSIONS

There is nothing more satisfying than enjoying a successful and fulfilling retirement. Now that we are living longer and healthier lives, we have the time to do the things we love. And we should most definitely be able to try new things. That is, we can reinvent and redefine ourselves. As I've indicated in my previous books, it is important to remain intellectually, socially, and physically active. It is imperative that we maintain our cognitive state as well as our mental well-being. I really do believe that you are never too old to learn something new. This process may take a bit longer, but you will be joyfully rewarded. The most critical first step is to actually try some new and exciting activities. In conjunction with the theme of this book, there are frugal ways to do this. Here are some suggestions.

Dancing
Some years back my wife and I became very interested in ballroom dancing. We began to take group lessons in a variety of frugal ways. Those venues included programs offered by local park and recreation departments. These programs are usually hosted by instructors from local dance studios. You end up with quality lessons at a fraction of the studio price. We've also found that most dance studios that offer weekend dances preface those dances with group lessons at no additional cost. For example, the studios where we dance in the Phoenix area, present a ninety-minute lesson followed by a three-hour ballroom dance. We've found the group dance lessons to be just

as effective as the more costly private lessons. The total cost for all of this is usually five dollars. We continue to dance on a regular basis attending dance parties that are offered by these local dance studios and disc jockeys. In the process, we have also made lots of new friends.

I suggest that you search online for local studios including *arthurmurray.com* and *fredastaire.com* since they have the most franchises. Additionally, check your local dance studios for similar functions.

Log onto *ehow.com*. This site is full of instructional videos that are presented sequentially. You can learn practically every dance including belly dancing, fox-trot, the Hora, Charleston, and even hip-hop. I must admit, we did indeed learn some great waltz moves here. *Ballroomdancers.com* offers extensive free video lessons as well as music samples.

You may also want to check out YouTube. There are a plethora of dance instruction videos available. Simply type in the particular dance you are interested in and the video selection will appear. For example, I searched salsa dance steps and thousands of videos appeared. Interestingly, many of the videos presented are put together by professional instructors.

Acting
Have you ever acted? Perhaps you've been on stage previously? You may be interested in pursuing the art of acting, as it will effect your personal development and socialization.

Many communities have amateur theater groups that offer workshops or classes. You can check at your local library or nearby college for classes. Many amateur performance venues do not require any particular skills. People of all ages and abilities are readily accepted. Check out the American Association of Community Theatre (*aact.org*) for a variety of useful resources.

Bicycling

I have been an avid biker for at least thirty years. It all began when my wife and I were RVing in our motorhome and my bike came with us. Then, in 1995 we bought a tandem bike and have been doing this ever since. Depending on how energetic we feel, some of our rides can be quite challenging.

We now own two tandem bicycles. We keep one at each of our residences. Biking has become an integral part of our lifestyle, especially during the retirement years. The benefits are numerous. And, if you check online listings such as Craigslist, you can easily purchase a frugally-priced bike. Our second tandem was in like-new condition and cost only $200.

The exercise is great, especially on rides of longer duration. You will also appreciate the scenery around you more so than driving. You will also reduce air pollution and save on your fuel cost. Take some bungee cords or a set of panniers (the bags that hang on the sides of your wheels) and you can easily handle short trips to the market, picnics, and various sporting events. The cost of parking will also be eliminated. And, we especially enjoy the socialization while riding on the tandem. We basically share the experience. If you have a rack for your bike, a whole new realm of exploration can open up to you. You can park your car and take off. We take our tandems with us everywhere. At our Arizona location, we especially enjoy biking through the splendid state and national parks. If you really get hooked on biking you might try longer-term bike trips.

Check out *bicyclinglife.com* for some great ideas about to get started, practical tips, and suggestion for practical cycling (everyday errands).

Camping

After 42 years of camping and RVing, I can tell you this is a great way to save money and enjoy the beauty of our country. In fact, in my previous book, *RVing and Your Retirement Lifestyle*, I explore in detail the advantages of doing so.

We are surrounded by beautiful state and national parks that are awaiting your arrival. There are a variety of ways to explore these attractions. Indeed, you can rough it and camp in a tent and sleeping bag.

You can also check in to a fully-equipped campground with a variety of amenities including a fitness center, pool, and a clubhouse. If you do not own a recreational vehicle, it is an easy matter to rent one or even stay in a cabin. In fact, many RV parks offer on-site rentals. Those would include travel trailers and motorhomes. In the long run, the RV lifestyle does truly get back to nature and can save you money.

Check out the following websites:

- *gocampingamerica.com*
- *camping-usa.com*
- *nps.gov*

Writing

Do you think that you have talent as a writer? If you've had any inkling to write, why not give it a shot? There are many venues. In addition to the traditional avenues such as newspapers, magazines, book publishers, and journals, there is the Internet and print on demand (POD). These tools of technology offer you the opportunity to get your writing into the public domain quickly and easily.

POD offers you the choice of getting your work out there without the challenges of gaining the interest of a traditional publisher.

Have you ever thought about writing a memoir? It is a great way to reflect and record events of your life. A memoir can consist looking back at a short period of time, or, it can encompass a decade as well as an entire life. You probably will not be able to fit everything in, but the challenge is deciding what to leave out. It may be difficult to record 10 years of events from your life and consolidate them to three pages. Keep a notebook or journal handy that you've regularly scribbled notes in. When your memoir is completed, you may be able to publish it either through a traditional process or self-publishing.

You can begin the process by making a list of all the important dates and events in your life. Help the process by looking at old photos and journals. Begin writing after you gather the information.

As an example, I recently had a conversation with a friend of mine whose husband committed suicide. She decided to write a memoir inclusive of events that lead to their getting-together years ago up to the present day. She also wrote about her feelings in regards to what may have precipitated the final days of her husband's life.

Take Classes

As I've alluded to previously, taking classes at your local community center, library, or adult education program can be a rewarding way to save money and grow. Check your local newspaper or community bulletins to keep abreast of these classes. You can learn all sorts of new hobbies and in most cases, at very reasonable prices.

Cooking

Let's face it—we've all got to eat. Why not attempt to reinvent our cooking strategies.

You can revitalize your techniques in additional ways other than simply trying out a new recipe. How about using different ingredients? Perhaps you can try new spices or tools such as a panini grill, a steamer, or a slow cooker.

In our home, we eat a variety of ethnic foods. Oftentimes, ideas come to us from sampling items from menus at restaurants. In addition, if you have friends that enjoy cooking, you might want to start a cooking club. You can even take classes in adult education programs in your town and it can also be very helpful to watch a variety of cooking shows.

Collecting

When you think about it, you can collect almost anything. Some of the more popular items are baseball cards, coins, stamps, seashells, and even doorknobs, cans, and wire.

Collecting can be about anything that interests you. It is a hobby that you clearly learn from. You have the desire to build something very special that means a great deal to you.

In addition, the process of collecting can be a challenge. Many collectors go to auctions, garage sales, and flea markets.

Here some examples along with websites:

- bottles (*fohbc.com*)
- buttons (*iwantbuttons.com/NBS*)
- baskets (*basketmakers.com*)
- autographs (*autographcollector.com*)
- comic art forms (*comicbooks.about.com*)

Genealogy

There are many interesting questions that can be answered with a bit of genealogical research. You may be interested in your family heritage. Studying your family tree can lead to very interesting results regarding kinship and family pedigree background. The results of your research and prove to be satisfying.

Most genealogists begin their research by collecting family documents and stories. A foundation is created for document research, which involves examining records about ancestors.

You may be able to collect data from older relatives. Find out as much information as possible about names of ancestors, dates of birth, and places where these people lived. Your public library may be a good place to begin. You can also visit *ancestry.com* and *ancestorhunt.com.*

Mygenealogysecrets.com offers a free mini-course on genealogy. This is a ten-part email course.

Volunteering

In my most recent book, *Volunteering & Your Retirement Lifestyle*, I emphasize with great zeal the fact that this is the time to reinvent, rediscover, and redefine yourself. In consideration of the variety of ways you can volunteer, perceiving volunteering as a hobby is easy to understand. So, for example, if you are interested in archaeology, you may be able to find work at a museum or university. If you are interested in teaching, literacy volunteering may be for you. In fact, *experiencorps.org* pays 1800 older adults small stipends to tutor school children in 14 cities. They must work at least 15 hours per week.

If you have a pet, you may be able to use your pet for pet therapy at an assisted-living facility or nursing home.

A very important consideration for you is to think about how much time you are willing to devote to your interest. You do indeed want your assignment to be meaningful and a learning experience.

If you have an artistic talent, others can learn from you. My wife and I are veteran musicians who love to play. It is our hobby. In fact, we met playing in a band. We enjoy playing to such an extent that we volunteer to entertain others at senior centers, or other recreation programs.

See the chapter in this book on frugal travel ideas for information regarding volunteer vacations.

I suggest that you check out RSVP (Retired Seniors Volunteer Program). This is a volunteer program offered by Senior Corps (*seniorcorps.gov*). RSVP is a large volunteer network for people over the age of 55. Opportunities are available through thousands of local and national organizations. The organization offers pre-service training and training from the organization you serve. You can readily choose how and where you want to serve. The website's "get involved" link allows you to search by areas of interest and by locations.

Cross-Cultural Solutions (*crossculturalsolutions.org*) volunteer programs are well suited to retirees who would like to share their life experiences with people around the world. They have supported more than 25,000 volunteers in their quest for a love of learning and exploration. You will find 1–12 week programs in Africa, Asia, Eastern Europe, or Latin America. At their website, you can read amazing testimonials or volunteers who have participated in programs around the world.

As previously mentioned, my wife and I volunteer for Heifer International (*heifer.org*). Their main goal is to work towards ending world hunger and caring for the earth by providing sustainable gifts of livestock and agricultural training. They offer programs in community volunteering and as well as activities at their learning centers. We have done a number of presentations at public schools through their Read to Feed Program. Needless to say, these experiences offer a great deal to the participant in terms of learning. Please check out their website for the latest offerings.

If you have the desire to volunteer but have limited financial resources and may not be able to afford traveling expenses, then perhaps you should consider virtual volunteering. If you are not familiar with the term, it refers to completing volunteer tasks in whole or in part via the Internet. Certainly, for you to be successful at this type of volunteering you will need to be somewhat technologically savvy. I suggest that you should also consider the following:

- Do you have regular and consistent access to the Internet.
- Do you communicate will via the written word?
- Can you stick to a deadline?
- Are you okay working on your own without direct supervision?
- Do you pace yourself well?

Virtual volunteering is a great way to give back to nonprofit organizations, schools, government agencies, and other agencies that utilize volunteer services.

VOLUNTEER PROFILE

The following example illustrates how you can utilize your skills to give back.

Don Chiapetti – In 2011 this man, a retired dentist, donated 81 musical instruments to schools. These days, school systems may be experiencing difficult economic circumstance that make it difficult to obtain instruments. He is committed to helping arts programs in schools. He maintains a network of musical instrument repairmen. In addition, he constantly seeks out instrument donations from various sources.

Hiking

There is nothing more satisfying than being in surrounded by nature.

Previous to writing this, I returned from a glorious hike in the McDowell Preserve in Fountain Hills, Arizona. Hiking does indeed have an amazing effect on your mind, body, and spirit, which does lead to a more positive perspective.

Hiking trails are available in every state. Many hikers begin at home visiting trails that may have been the site of former railroads and have been converted to hiking and biking trails. You can find a trail that will meet your needs in terms of physical ability, and present appropriate challenges.

A very informative website is *traildino.com*. Here you will find an extensive database of trails around the world accompanied by a variety of pictures and reviews. You can also log onto *railstotrails.org* to locate former rail trails. *Trails.com* has a good trail locator link along with topographic maps. The site also rates the best trails in North America.

Reading

Reading is one of life's great joys. It is so invigorating to be able to see the world, whether fictional or not, through another person's eyes. Think about the possibilities that await you. You can travel, meet new people, learn about new gourmet delights, experience new relationships, enhance your knowledge of history, art, politics, and a plethora of other subjects. And, you can do this without leaving the comfort of your home. Perhaps you will be stimulated enough to travel and continue the learning process.

Here are some suggestions:

- Join or form a book club to you can share your joy of reading with others.
- Read as much as you can by one author and become an expert.
- Read books from the best-seller lists in an effort to stimulate lively discussions.

Check out *modernlibrary.com* for up to date information about suggestions for reading novels and other literature.

A great way to read frugally and to clear your bookshelves of books you will never read again is as follows: Swap your books through *paperbackswap.com*. After registering at the website, post at least 10 books that you are willing to swap. This process will get you 2 book credits that you can use to request books from other members. With more than 3 million books available you will surely find something you want to read. Other members pay the postage to send you books. In return, you ship your posted books when requests come in. Remember; this process will help to de-clutter your home. It will also provide you with free presents for family and friends and gives you the chance to trade regular print books for large-print versions.

Do not forget all the possibilities you have these days at your local library. Your card may allow you to check out the following (in addition to books):

- e-books
- magazines
- audio-books

It may also allow you to access certain electronic collections. Be sure to check out the library website.

Photography

One of the most popular frugal hobbies for those of us over the age of 55 is photography. You can basically purchase as much or as little equipment as you desire.

In this digital age, photos can be taken, downloaded, and viewed immediately. The new cameras have transformed a previously expensive hobby to one that is affordable. In addition, they can be stored by various software programs on your computer hard drive, or, they can be posted online for free by such websites as *Facebook.com, picasa.google.com, or flickr.com.* Or you can fill up a memory stick or card with a great many pictures. Then, you can print the ones you like and discard the ones you don't. As you probably know, it is quite easy to share you photos through email.

Certainly, if you prefer doing things the old-fashioned way, as many of us do, actually developing your own prints can be quite satisfying. As retirees, we do have the time to devote to our hobbies Learning about the procedures for darkroom technology can be fascinating. You can even begin your new hobby by taking classes at your local college or even your local adult education program.

Some examples of subject matter can include landscapes, portraits, history, nudes, abstraction, and the human condition.

By the way, be sure to visit the About.com (*photography.about.com*) photography website. You will be presented with a free course on all-important aspects introducing you to photography.

Art

In general, art encompasses a very broad area. It can include painting, etching, sketching, sculpture, architecture, textiles, jewelry, and crayon drawing.

Your focus should be on narrowing down your activities to specific areas of interest. A great way to start is to study the brochures from local enrichment programs offered by local colleges and parks and recreation departments, and adult education programs. You can experiment to see where your passions lie.

Another approach is to study some art history, which you can do through a museum or your local library.

Some examples of art periods as suggested by Kevin Price in his book, *The Successful Retirement Guide,* include:

- Primitive – rock carvings, cave paintings
- Ancient and classical Greece
- Byzantine
- Renaissance
- Baroque

- Modern

If you log onto the AARP (*aarp.org/personal-growth*) website, you will find a free online course entitled "Expressive Drawing Curriculum." You are presented with a 12-session program including lessons on drawing a portrait of your inner self, drawing to the beat, and drawing on the edge.

At Free Online Art Classes (*free-online-art-classes.com*) you can take courses in painting, drawing, collage, oil pastels, colored pencils, printmaking, basic drawing, jewelry making, fabric printing, and much more. There are also a variety of videos that you can watch to enhance the learning experience. There is even a section on art therapy that enables people to cope with a variety of challenges. In addition, you will also find links to artful cooking, artful lighting, and artful gardening.

Gardening

As I'm sure you know, the more fruits and vegetables you eat, the healthier you'll be. Take it from a long-time vegetarian—it does work. And, if you maintain your own garden, you will be very pleased with the "fruits" of your labor. Take it from a long-time gardener.

The produce from your own garden always seems to be tastier than the produce that is purchased from a market. Furthermore, you will have exact control over how your garden grows. Ultimately, this is a frugal hobby.

Some frugal gardening tips are as follows:

- Try to save seeds. That would involve collecting seeds from your self-pollinating plants as well as seeds that you purchase commercially. Remember, you can purchase seeds at discount stores such as Dollar Stores. In fact, many of these discount outlets sell vegetable plants. I purchase the majority of my vegetable garden plants from the Save and Discount store near me.

- You can divide existing plants into additional plants.
- Check classified listings such as Craigslist and local newspapers for free plants.
- Keep a watchful eye on catalog promotions that may allow you your first order free.
- Sign-up for store mailing lists in an effort to be aware of promotions.
- Make your own garden supplies such as potting mix and even seed pots from newspaper.
- Consider creating a garden with a friend, neighbor, or family member. With the joint effort, the cost will be less, the maintenance shared, and the outcome bountiful.

Sewing and Crafting

If you love to sew, why not use your free time to make clothes and other items that you would normally purchase. Useful sewing projects could include making your own napkins, repairing towels, mending your clothing, making your own grocery bags, and hemming pants.

Money-saving crafters make gifts, home decorating items, and even jewelry. A great place to begin is your local thrift shop where you can buy used items that may supply fabric for a project that you have in mind. Or, perhaps you may be interested in buying some used candles, melting them down, and making your own candle creations.

CHAPTER 5: RESOURCEFUL ENTERTAINMENT OPTIONS

If you've worked many long and hard years, your goal now may be to play hard. Finding ways to entertain yourself does not necessarily mean that you have to spend a great deal of money. You may need to engage your creative side when choosing your entertainment options.

A large variety of interesting entertainment choices exists for retirees these days. And, you do not have to spend a great deal in the process.

If you reside in a town that has a senior center and or an active park and recreation department, be certain to check out their calendars. From dances to board games to a variety of trips, you will keep active. For example, my small town in Connecticut offers the following classes:

- tai chi
- line dancing
- ballroom dancing
- sewing and craft classes
- basketball

In addition, you can sign up for cooking classes with a local chef, and even take a coastal navigation course.

Then there are the simple obvious courses of action. When you go to the movies, attend the opening of a museum exhibit, or even book a vacation, make sure that you enquire about the senior discounts. Many cities and towns have dollar movie theatres. That works well if you do not mind seeing a movie a few weeks after everyone has. Furthermore, you can readily avoid the high-priced movie times by going to a matinee during the weekdays or weekends and bringing along your own treats. These are simple examples of ways to enjoy your frugal retirement.

Bankrate.com has come up with some suggestions for frugal entertainment. The following are some examples:

1. Attend community events. Be sure to get added to the mailing list of your local city or county newsletter that lists upcoming events. (Often times colleges and universities that receive public funding offer a wide range of events and services at little or no cost to the general public).
2. shows and performances offered locally
3. factory and business tours
4. Participate in library events. Local libraries offer many free events open to the public, such as concerts, lectures, and movies. Check the event calendar at the library website. Author events are very common.
5. Letterboxing – a modern family treasure hunt
6. Download or watch on-demand movies, obtain cheap seasonal passes, or look into discounted admissions for certain days of the week at theatres. Most theatres will allow you to purchase passes in bulk. This will save you money throughout the year. Also, think about joining a movie club.
7. Visit pick-your-own-farms where you can save some money and have fun. Many of these farms offer corn mazes, hayrides, and other family activities. This would be a great choice if you have grandchildren.
8. Enjoy local parks. They make for interesting walks, scenic bike rides, and nice picnics.
9. Attend local fairs. Do not forget to research less expensive admission for a fair.

10. Have fun at home. Try a new recipe in the kitchen, play board games, have a potluck dinner with friends, or start a comedy improv group. You can also dig out those board games and challenge your friends and family.
11. Get low-cost admissions to museums. Many museums provide a free day of access for the public, or at least a discounted day. In addition, there may be a variety of events taking place that you can attend. Again, check the website.

As suggested above, be certain that you check the available resources at your local library. My local library in Arizona offers an incredible selection of DVD and Blu-Ray discs. In fact, I've seriously considered dropping my Netflix membership.

By the way, community events can encompass of variety of venues. Your local library may have a calendar of events available to the public for no cost. In addition, you can also attend sporting events at your local high school for free. Their dramatic and musical productions are usually very reasonably priced and are lots of fun. I know this because I often play in the orchestra for the musicals. My wife and I recently attended a performance of Evita, the musical, at our local high school. The quality of the performance was excellent and the ticket prices were quite reasonable.

In addition, check your local newspaper for literary readings. Also, authors go on tours to promote their books at local bookstores. You would have a chance to meet the author and become familiar with their new work.

During periods of nice weather, many communities offer you the opportunity to attend free lunchtime concerts. If you pack a picnic lunch, you'll have a great way to enjoy the sunshine and the music.

If you like to read, you could join or create a book club or discussion group. These groups are a great way to exchange ideas and gain new perspectives.

How about a game night? You probably still have some board games in your house. Most likely, your friends also have some games. Invite them over for some frugal entertainment in the form of an inexpensive game night. My wife and I have recently begun playing Scrabble again via the traditional board way. Or, if you are adventurous, you can play Scrabble and other games online. Check out *games.com* or *pogo.com* or even Yahoo games (*games.yahoo.com).* Yahoo offers a large variety of games for you to participate in. Some are free of charge.

Another interesting idea is to attend gallery openings and art walks. We often times go to the Scottsdale Arizona Thursday evening art walks in the Old Town area. Aside from the wine and hors d'oeuvres offerings, you have an opportunity to meet artists and gallery owners along with other art lovers when you tour local galleries on the same evening.

If you enjoy watching movies, and you have the ability to stream, Netflix streams movies on an unlimited basis for only $8 a month. You can also view free shows at *Hulu.com,* *TVClassicShows.com,* and *TVLand.com.* In addition, you can pick up a film at Redbox kiosks for only $1 and those can be reserved online at redbox.com. When you are done you can return the DVD to any Redbox kiosk nationwide. At the time of this writing, there is also Blockbuster Express, which offers $1 DVD rentals. Given the nature of Blockbuster's financial difficulties, their future may be uncertain.

Another frugal alternative to movie rental fees are video resources available from your public library. You may not realize the extent of DVD (many with Blu-ray format) movies you can borrow. I have been thinking about cancelling my DVD membership to Netflix because of both the cost and the amount of time I often have to wait to receive a title. I was astounded not only when I discovered the number of DVDs available at the library, but also the wonderful system of inter-library lending that is in place. If I request a movie and it is not in, I only have to wait a short amount of time for it to be shipped from another branch. You are readily able to keep a steady stream of DVDs on your queue at the library. In most cases you have a week before you have to return the items.

There are several websites that offer free movies. You will do best with this alternative if you have a high-speed Internet connection. Those sites include:

- *hulu.com*
- *snagfilms.com*
- *vech.com*

Internet radio stations such as nu Tsie, StereoMood, and Jango offer music to fit your taste and mood. Radio Tuna searches for online stations currently streaming the artist or genre you've requested. A main advantage that Internet radio stations have is that you do not need to be techno-savvy. It is very similar to traditional radio if you have wireless Internet in your home.

AARP (*aarp.org*)

I've been a member of AARP for at least thirty years. If you do not belong, you should join immediately. Aside from discounts on auto insurance, travel, and shopping in general, you will learn about fabulous opportunities for entertainment.

A recent check of the Entertainment link indicated a community movie group that you can join in an effort to learn about new movies that are hot at the box office. You can join a discussion group or even create your own.

The game link offers a variety of arcade, sports, card, and word games that you can easily play online.

Additional entertainment options include book discussions and reviews, arts and music videos and activities, and opportunities to participate in a various leisure activities.

Great Deals on Concert Tickets and Shows Online

If you have some flexibility, and you would like to be frugal with your entertainment budget, there are some websites that can readily save you some money.

SeatGeek.com predicts the best time to purchase tickets for concerts or sporting events. If you sign up for their email list, they will let you know when and if the prices drop.

I've also used *showuptickets.com* to buy tickets for theatre productions in Arizona. Unsold tickets are sold at greatly reduced prices. Basically, you simply insert your locale and the available events and tickets appear.

You can also check for tickets on Craigslist just as long as you can verify the authenticity of the seller.

iTunes Store

The iTunes Store is a great frugal way to entertain yourself. You can download books at a cost of nothing up to around $10, along with movies, TV shows, and of course, music. The downloads are readily compatible with all Mac and Windows-based platforms. You would simply need to download and install the iTunes software, establish an account, and you are ready to be entertained. If you have an iPhone, iPod, or iPad, you can obtain apps directly from the iTunes store, many of which are free. The store has over 150,000 podcasts available for subscription as well as 20,000 hours of audiobooks.

Free Online Music Resources

The following sites offer free music to listen or download.

1. *pandora.com* – All you need to do is enter a favorite artist, composer, or song and the site will create custom radio stations featuring your favorite music.
2. *npr.com* – Here you can download songs and concerts
3. *spinner.com* – Choose from 350 radio stations and download the free MP3 of the day.
4. *jango.com* – This site allows you to enter the artist's name and it will play songs by that artist. You can even create your own custom playlist.
5. *billboard.com* – Listen to the top 100 songs on the billboard charts or, check out new releases.
6. *amazon.com* – Choose from over 1000 songs that are available for free download.
7. Free Napster – This is the no-cost companion to *napster.com*. You can listen to each song three times and up to 25 times each month.

Out to Dinner the Frugal Way

My wife and I love to dine out. We enjoy eating a variety of food. What we would prefer not to do is to spend more than we have to. Here are some suggestions that will save you money.

A very popular website is *restaurant.com*. The site attempts to introduce people to new restaurants and offers patrons the simple of pleasure of eating good food. You can readily try new cuisines at a very reasonable price. At the website you type in your ZIP code, and then you are presented with restaurants that offer coupons for various amounts. Typically, we purchase $25 certificates for $2 or $50 certificates for $4 during their promotions. This is a great way to save money.

The authors of *Retiring on a Poor Man's Budget* suggest the following ideas to save money when dining out:

- Look for restaurants with early-bird specials or senior discounts.
- Go out to breakfast or lunch rather than dinner.
- If you take your grandchildren, find a restaurant with a children's menu or "kids eat free" night.
- Clip a coupon from your local newspaper or the Internet.
- Skip the appetizer and dessert.
- Keep close tabs on your drinks tab.

Some other common sense tips to save money include:
- Avoid over-ordering.
- Order only what you actually think you will eat.
- Drink regular water.

If you are not a big eater, there is nothing wrong with sharing a meal. Simply ask for an extra plate to accompany your order.

Inquire about restaurant specials. A special may simply mean something that is featured and not necessarily discounted.

If you have an AAA card, offer to show it. That may bring an additional discount.

CHAPTER 6: FRUGAL TRAVEL IDEAS

Earlier in this book I alluded to the fact that since we are living longer and healthier lives, we can reinvent ourselves and rediscover our inner passions.

As we our now in our Third Age—that period of time after raising a family and work—we may have dreams. One of those dreams may be to get out and see the world. If you are living under budget constraints, you do not necessarily have to be tied down to your home. There are a variety of ways to travel. These days, airlines, hotels, scenic attractions, and other vendors do indeed offer incentives to attract seniors. The key here is to be able to find these deals. The most important consideration in the early stages of planning is to come up with a budget. Then you will need to decide where you'd like to go.

My wife and I travel both domestically and internationally. Over the years I have learned to utilize certain frugal strategies that have limited unnecessary spending and allowed us to gain the most from our financial resources.

If part of your long-term plan during retirement is to travel, and you would like to make the most of your money, then perhaps you should consider these ideas that *bankrate.com* has put forth.

- Divulge Your True Age - Be certain that you broadcast your true age whenever you get the opportunity to that you can take advantage of all senior discounts. Utilize those AAA and AARP cards. Indeed, they do offer all kinds of travel discounts. Many hotel chains offer senior discount programs. Some even offer a 50 percent discount.

- Explore Airpasses – An airpass allows you to fly to multiple destinations within a country or region for one set price. You can also purchase an airpass for multi-country visits. As an aside, the editors of Budget Travel Magazine recommend the Jetblue airpass as the best all-around. This pass allows unlimited travel for a 30-day period for a cost of around $700.
- Take a Tour – A great way to save money is to join a tour group. Those may include alumni associations, church and retirement community travel groups, and even municipal senior or park and recreation travel groups. Remember, you are getting a group discount on everything from entrance fees to hotel rooms. In my previous books I discuss the wonders of Elderhostel *(roadscholar.org)*. This organization offers nearly 8,000 lifelong learning adventures for those of us over 55 in all states and over 50 countries. Programs are offered in conjunction with educational institutions, museums, national parks, performing arts centers and others. Most fees are all-inclusive. At the time of this writing there were a variety of programs offered for less than $600.

Let's examine some other frugal travel suggestions:

House Swapping
If you have a condo with a fantastic city skyline view, why not swap it for a vacation with someone who has a place overlooking a Caribbean beach. House swapping as been referred to as one of most pronounced ways of getting a feel for wherever you travel. Intervac International *(intervac.com)* offers listings in at least 50 countries. They suggest a vacation duration of between 2 and 4 weeks. The website offers a variety of listing pictures. Advantages of doing this include the

elimination of hotel and maybe even car rental expenses, immersion into another culture's lifestyle, and the security and comfort of living at home while being on holiday.

AARP has come up with some basic principles to assist you in finding the best swap.

1. Make a wish. Think about what you would like in a home including things like air conditioning, water view, and a garden.
2. Learn the lingo. You may think of the word villa as referring to an estate in the bucolic countryside. Europeans may think of this word as a small house on the edge of town.
3. Check your assumptions. A house that sleeps eight might not mean four bedrooms as much as four beds in one room.
4. Ask some questions. Ask things like what do you see when you look out the windows of your house? Do an exchange of interior and exterior photos.
5. Get references, especially from other families that may have exchanged previously with your perspective swap.
6. Start early. AARP suggests that you begin your search nine to twelve months in advance of your travel. For summer exchanges you'll want to have your home listed by the previous fall.

They also offer some timely advice:
- Set some rules. What about responsibility for cleaning and laundry? What about car swapping? (If you do this, make sure that the registration is available.)
- Cover your bases. A list should be made available regarding quirks of the houses you swap. Also, compile a list of local restaurants and sightseeing opportunities.

Ask your swap partner to do the same. Enlist the help of a neighbor to assist your guests with the inevitable questions they may have.

- Keep out. Agree ahead of time about things like contents of the refrigerator, and what is off limits.

Vacation Home Rentals

Renting another families' home has become more popular in recent years. The main reason for this is that it is a frugal alternative. There's that word again!

Often times you can save money over hotel costs because you do not incur service charges or gratuities and you have more space. That is, you have a kitchen and a living room and perhaps even a private pool or a hot tub. And, you have the advantage of renting in a more rural location. Many vacation rentals give travelers the option of inhabiting real neighborhoods in their destination and living like the local residents.

Rental properties include homes, cottages, condominiums or town homes.

There are many agencies that rent properties. One of the most reliable is VRBO (*vrbo.com*). That stands for Vacation Rentals by Owner. They feature 160,000 rentals in over 100 countries worldwide. You find comparisons to hotel rates at the site with general savings indicators. You will also find a variety of reviews with links to Facebook and Twitter. Clark Howard, the money expert from CNN, suggests that you look for places that were recently built and have lots of pictures posted online. Both of these considerations will help insure that the rental will be in very good condition. And, request additional pictures beyond what is posted online, which will help you be more certain about what you are renting.

Vacation Apartment Rentals

An increasingly popular idea is to rent apartments for vacations. My wife and I recently returned from an extended trip to Italy.

In Rome, we rented a beautiful apartment, fully furnished with all amenities from Rental in Rome (*rentalinrome.com*). The building was centrally located and we felt right at home. There were four of us that shared the accommodations. We actually prepared many of our own meals.

This vacation apartment rental was very reasonably priced in comparison to pricey hotels in the area of downtown Rome. Travelers searching for this type of value and the enjoyment of a neighborhood experience now have a variety of choices among city apartments being offered as short-term vacation rentals. Due to a stagnating real estate market, many owners who would otherwise prefer to sell are renting in an effort to make ends meet. Be certain to check out websites such as AirBnB, Homeaway, and TripAdvisor. You can also conduct a specific online search of available rentals in the area you are interested in.

Additional Vacation Rental Sites

In a recent issue of Budget Travel Magazine, the writers discussed some of the country's largest vacation rental sites.

- Homeaway (*homeaway.com*) – With 325,000 listings at the time of this writing, this site offers the largest selection. The process allows you to compare up to 5 rentals at one time.
- Airbnb (*airbnb.com*) – The site specializes in long-term rentals and last-minute options along with some offbeat spaces including yachts.
- Flipkey (*flipkey.com*) – This is a highly rated site that lists points of interests near the specific property.

- Wyndham (*wyndhamrentals.com*) – Here you will find high-end hand selected rentals in North America and Europe.

Time-Share Rentals

Time-share owners may often look to rent their slots. A common source for locating these rentals can be Craigslist. You can also locate rentals by the week, or night, at *resortime.com*, *evrentals.com/* or *condodirect.com.* These sites can save you as much as 35% off of regular fees.

Know Where to Look For the Best Travel Deals

These days, there are a large number of general online travel resources. Those sites include Travelocity, Expedia, Hotwire, Priceline, Orbitz, and even Costco.

There are just as many sites that specialize in discount airfare and airfare comparison. Those include Bing, Farecompare, Airfarewatchdog, and *Fly.com.* Be certain to compare all the sites since they have different electronic reservation systems.

Consumers Reports Magazine suggests that you begin your searching for flights at least 3½ months before the departure date. That is when the market begins to sort itself out. Many airline and travel sites make it simple to set up alerts to track prices. The magazine offers some additional suggestions:

- Try to buy seats on Tuesday afternoons as most sale periods begin on Monday evenings and end Thursday evenings.
- Be wary of booking on weekends.
- Consider a connecting flight to save money.
- Try not to book flights within 14 days of departure.

The travel sites begin the process of pointing you in the right directions. But, there are some caveats. First, they only reflect the prices of vendors that chose to be included on their sites and pay appropriate fees. At the time of this writing, Expedia and Hotwire chose to drop American Airlines from its sites over such a fee dispute.

I have found that in many instances, you will find lower costs if you go directly to the airline or cruise ship company or hotel to book. Many airlines are now looking cut out the middlemen and lower costs to the consumer. I do most of my domestic flying on Southwest Airlines. They do not participate in any of the travel websites' directories. Their airfares are always very reasonable. Furthermore, there are no baggage fees and they do not charge customers to change nonrefundable tickets. They also have a simple boarding process, which becomes even easier if you check-in online the day before you travel. Other discount airlines that are recommended by USA today include Frontier, Hawaiian, and Alaska Airlines.

Believe it or not, there are times when you can save more money by not going online to book flights. Remember the days when you would actually talk to live people called travel agents. Well, there are actually instances when a real person can offer you cost saving alternatives in terms of routes and other travel advice and make suggestions that computer counterparts cannot do. These savings can be especially noticeable on international flights. If you are flying domestically, do your research with online search engines such as *airfarewatchdog.com*. Also, check the Southwest Airlines (*southwest.com*) fares as they do not participate in those search engines. In addition, do not hesitate to seek out travel agents online with good reviews. A recent article in the New York Times suggests that the following agencies with online access are a good bet:

- BACC Travel (*bacctravel.com*)

- Bella's Travel (*bellastravel.com*)
- Pan Adriatic Travel (*panadriatic.com*)

If you have a list of hotels that you are interested in, I recommend that you check with the hotel website or call them directly. Check out their specials for seniors, military personnel, or frequent travelers. Also, they may offer a better price if there are a large number of unoccupied rooms available.

By all means be certain to check the *tingo.com* website. If you book a hotel through them and the price of the room goes down, they will rebook the room at the lower price. If you book using a credit card, they will automatically refund the difference on your card. I really do not think you can find a more frugal process to book a hotel room.

Another helpful suggestion is subscribe to some online travel deal websites. For example, Travelzoo (*travelzoo.com*) has over 21 million subscribers who receive weekly emails relating great deals on vacation packages, cruises, hotels, and car rentals. Included in the newsletter are weekly "top 20" deals. Often times these deals reflect last minute attempts to fill vacancies. You can also check into weekly Hotwire (*hotwire.com*) deals newsletter. This site can keep a record of your travel preferences.

These days several airlines are offering same-day promo codes for frequent flier members. Indeed, it does make good sense to follow these feeds if you have the flexibility to go at the last minute. Travel experts say that normally seasonal deals for fall travel on airlines start to appear in August; for Christmas travel it is October. The more flexibility you have about when and where you want to travel, the more likely it is that you will find a great deal. I also suggest that you book quickly when a great deal appears since it may disappear quickly.

Jeff Yeager, author of *The Cheapskate Next Door,* surveyed some vacationers, and came up with some insightful tips:

- Many vacationers pay for most or even all of their vacations with mileage points, cash-back, or other travel awards that they earn throughout the year by using their credit cards for everything they purchase. (I do the same thing; I rarely ever pay for airfare).
- Off-season travel is usually when you will find the best bargains and smallest crowds.
- Contact the chambers of commerce and tourist information bureaus for the areas you will be visiting before you leave home. They may have discount offers and coupons available from local merchants.
- Buy an entertainment book for the area you will be visiting. You can save big money on dining using *restaurant.com* or, a two-for-one coupon book. (We do both and save big time).
- Enjoy lunch rather than dinner at that five-star restaurant you've wanted to try. You might save 30 to 50 percent on your bill.
- If you are traveling by car, consider renting rather than driving your own vehicle. Since most rental cars come with unlimited mileage, it may be to your advantage to do this if you plan on driving a lot of miles in a short period of time.

SAVE MONEY ON YOUR NEXT CRUISE

If you are considering cruising, Budget Travel Magazine suggests that working with a travel agent works best. Most agents have a close relationship with the cruise lines, which may mean that they be able to obtain upgrades and extras, such as two-for-one deals. You would not have access to those specials on your own. Those agents are paid commissions by the cruise lines so you will not have to pay for their help. They may also offer more insight and personal advice based on their personal experience. Try to find an agent that has been in business for at least 5 years. The magazine also suggests that you book that cruise six or more months in advance when many two-for-one deals are offered—or at the last minute. Most cruise lines do not want their ships to sail with unoccupied cabins. If you book in advance, you can usually negotiate the balance before the final payment is due.

Budget Travel also recommends that you purchase airfare on your own and not from the cruise ship company. You will save more money that way and have additional flexibility on travel times.

About 50 to 65 days before a sailing, cruise lines tend to reduce retail prices by 20% to fill those unsold cabins. However, those deals may only last for two or three days. Again, last minute decision-making may come into play. Do not hesitate to subscribe to individual cruise line emails to find out about deals.

Be as flexible as possible on your sailing dates. Obviously, prices are at their highest during the holiday travel periods. Off-peak months such as May and September can be the most affordable months to cruise.

Often times a frugal alternative can be a repositioning cruise. Cruise lines sometimes move a ship from one cruising area to another, such as from the U.S. to Europe. Rates for these cruises can be much less than traditional itineraries. It is important to note that these trips can be longer than usual with a great deal more time spent at sea. So, they may not be a viable alternative for everyone.

Incidentally, sometimes premium cruise lines offer excellent deals on their high-end ships,

By all means take advantage of incentives. Cruise lines frequently roll out short-term incentives during the first few months of the year in an effort to lock in business. Those goodies can include onboard credits or even spa treatments.

If you have the flexibility to travel on a last-minute basis, a package can prove to be a frugal alternative. Hotel and flight combinations can end up costing less than a ticket alone since the package airfares are pre-arranged. Make certain that you log onto *lastminutetravel.com* for great deals.

By the way, you may be able to fly first class for almost the same price as a fully refundable coach fare. These fares are called Y-Ups and can be found on *kayak.com*.

Another suggestion for frugal travel is to travel off-season. The weeks before and after the most popular travel seasons can save you money on hotels and airfare. For example, the week before Thanksgiving is a good time to obtain cheaper airfare. Traveling to Europe in late fall or early winter can be cost effective as well. A good time to go to Las Vegas can be the week between Christmas and New Years.

Seasoned travelers frequently get good deals on hotels. I've learned to always check prices directly with the hotel or it's 800 number after I get prices from the discount websites. Always inquire about a cheaper price than the one you've been quoted. You may find that your AAA or AARP membership can substantially reduce costs. For example, the Hyatt Hotels and Resorts senior discount can be as much as 50 percent. Make sure that you explore additional benefits such as free breakfasts, free parking, and discounts on local recreation.

Volunteer Vacations (Voluntourism)

In the Frugal Hobbies chapter I espouse the virtues of volunteering as a hobby. In my previous book, *Volunteering &*

Your Retirement Lifestyle, I describe in detail the virtues of volunteer vacations. Basically, you combine traditional travel with volunteer work. In essence, you are taking a service-based vacation. You will find that there are many adventure travel companies that offer these trips. I suggest that you log onto adventuretravel.about.com to learn about voluntourism and explore many of the available opportunities. They offer an interesting link to assist you in deciding whether voluntourism is for you. By the way, this can be a great opportunity for a rewarding family endeavor, particularly if you have grandchildren.

Basically, you would be deeply rewarded spending a few hours per day giving back to your favorite nonprofit organization. In consideration for doing this, you most often are provided with free food and lodging as well as plenty of time for hiking, wildlife viewing, fishing, photography, and making new friends. Of course, another major advantage is the opportunity to immerse yourself in the culture of the people you are helping, especially if you volunteer overseas. If you are not into nature activities or are not in the greatest physical condition, there are many organizations of a cultural nature, such as museums, that offer similar programs.

If you are in good physical condition and feel adventurous, you can check out the Snake River Lodge and Spa in Jackson, Wyoming. At the time of this writing, you could secure a $385 room for $192 a night if you are willing to spend part of your vacation taking down barbed wire fences so local wildlife can roam more freely.

The frugal nature of this type of vacationing can offer the volunteer little or no cost other than getting to the site on your own.

The Colorado Trail Foundation (*coloradotrail.org*) cares for the Colorado Trail. They charge around $60 per week. World Wide Opportunities on Organic Farms (*wwoof.org*) offers opportunities to share sustainable ways of living. The cost can be as little as $30 per week.

Global Volunteers (*globalvolunteers.org*) offers short-term volunteers a volunteer vacation either domestically or internationally from 1 to 3 weeks in length. They have been mobilizing over 27,000 volunteers on 6 continents since 1984.

I would also suggest that you log onto *volunteerabroadfree.com* to explore opportunities to teach abroad, volunteer in orphanages, and volunteer in such countries as India, Africa, and Nepal. This organization works with a variety of international groups that are willing to pay volunteers a small salary or provide free room and board for helping with their cause. Healthcare professionals are especially needed abroad, particularly in poverty-stricken countries.

Road Scholar (formerly Elderhostel) offers wonderful programs such as Navajo Nation Schools in Arizona. This popular program has two 6-night programs where travelers assist children and teachers in Navajo Reservation schools. You will learn about the Navajo culture, take a field trip, and enjoy evening lectures and entertainment. The cost is less than $700, which is a bargain. And, you will be near many Southwestern attractions such as the Grand Canyon. Road Scholar has many other service programs such as archaeological preservation. This organization serves members over the age of 50.

OTHER VOLUNTEER/TRAVEL ORGANIZATIONS

FlyforGood.com - This organization offers an online trip finder that connects volunteers with humanitarian nonprofit organizations that are watched by nonprofit watchdog associations. The site also offers discounts of 10 to 25 percent off of published rates. Their goal is to make it more accessible and cheaper so more people can volunteer.

Travelocity Travel For Good
(*travelocity.com/TravelForGood*)
Several affordable volunteer travel partners including the American Hiking Society, which, at the time of this writing, offers week-long train maintenance trips for $250 that include rugged accommodations and food. They also award eight $5,000 grants annually to volunteer vacationers.

The Appalachian Mountain Club (*outdoors.org*) - offers a variety of trail cleanup programs in locations ranging from the White Mountains to the Virgin Islands for as low as $220 per week. The price covers meals and rustic lodging which includes cabins, canvas tents on platforms, or bunkhouses.

In addition, you may be able to get a super-cheap vacation from the AMC on St. John for $330 a week. Volunteers on this project would work around 4 to 6 hours a day carrying 20 pounds of tools and materials, clearing drainage ditches, cutting back vegetation, and building rock stairs. Normally, your afternoons would be free to swim, snorkel, and simply lounging on the beach.

Incidentally, the AMC website offers links for the 50+ age group which lists volunteer vacations that are less strenuous.

Cross-Cultural Solutions (*crossculturalsolutions.org*) - This organization offers a variety of one-week trips in eight different countries in additions to more traditional volunteer initiatives. Those countries include Brazil, Costa Rica, and Ghana. As part of its Insight Abroad program, volunteers were paid close to $2,000 last summer to paint schoolyards, plant vegetable gardens for the elderly, and work at daycare centers. Volunteers gain valuable insight into various cultures.

The Sierra Club (*sierraclub.org*) – The club runs 80 to 90 volunteer vacations per year. As well, they donate roughly 25,000 worker hours to state and federal land agencies. Prices for participants can range from $325 for a 6-day habitat restoration project in Florida to $2000 for an 11-day service trip in Maui with condominium accommodations. You would also be able to snorkel, hike, and whale watch. Volunteers usually team up with forest service rangers for many restoration projects.

RV Care-A-Vanners (*habitat.org*) - This is a Habitat for Humanity program for RVers. When you volunteer with this program, you will receive free or low-cost RV parking. The programs run about two weeks. You can choose to participate in the actual building of a house, or you can be assigned to less strenuous activities.

Voluntourism.org offers dozens of volunteer programs in the US and around the world for those who wish to participate in volunteer travel. You could be an eco-tracker in Ecuador, or work in a small community in Nepal.

Traveling With Grandchildren and Other   Family Members
Wouldn't it be great if you could find a frugal way to travel with your whole family or at least your grandchildren? Let's face it. We do indeed need quality time with those little ones and these experiences can result in lasting memories. Additionally, parents get built-in babysitting and some needed time alone. Unfortunately, group travel can get expensive.

Based on average hotel and domestic airfare costs, you could easily spend $3,000 for a four-night trip for six people exclusive of food and activities. Good planning, however, can make a considerable difference.

Money Magazine makes the following suggestions for cost cutting strategies:

- Drive to your destination if you are in the "radius of efficiency." They feel that you will save money, as compared with flying, if you drive less than 400 miles and you are traveling with more than 2 people.
- Fly at the right time. Try not to fly during peak vacation times.
- Buy at the time. Book spring break tickets from early January to early February; shop for summer tickets no more than 3½ months out.
- Think outside the box. Renting a house or a condo can save money over multiple hotel rooms.
- Cut the price of activities and meals. Oftentimes, ticket prices can be reduced if you call ahead for group rates or check with AAA or AARP. Also, try to make lunch the main meal and then eat a light dinner. That may save you upwards of $10 per entrée.

Frugal Travel Apps

In case you are not familiar with the term, application software, also know as an app, is software that is designed to help the user perform a single or multiple related tasks. As opposed to system software, apps assist in the performance of tasks that benefit the user. Most often, these apps are utilized on smartphones. Again, in case you are not familiar with the term, these phones offer more advanced computing ability and connectivity than a basic cell phone.

The boom in smartphones has generally made life easier. There are thousands of apps available. I would like to discuss a few of those apps that are specifically geared towards travel. In particular, most apps are frugal by nature.

The number of travel apps these days numbers in the thousands. Apps allow you to make bookings at a bargain price as well as check restaurant reviews on the fly. Many speak in foreign languages, help you find a restroom, verify taxi fares, as well as find cheap airfares and hotel accommodations. Some apps are free and some cost a minimal amount. Here are a few of the more popular apps depending on which smartphone you own.

- Kayak – Kayak finds cheap flights, rooms, and package trips and is free.
- Gateguru – This app has maps of 86 U.S. airports and will help you find a gate, and find something to eat in most airports.
- Hotels.com – With 80,000 member hotels, discount room rates abound.
- Aroundme – Lists key services (food, gas, etc.) closest to your current location.
- Curcon – Currency converter app.
- Free Translator – Loaded with 35 languages, this app translates your phrases and says it out loud.
- iCruise – With more than 12,000 itineraries on more than 20 cruise lines, this new cruise finder app has one of the largest listing databases out there along with lots of other features. You can also check out detailed cabin photos.
- Always Be Cruising – Here you can connect with other cruisers and get advice on many aspects of cruising.

- Ship Mate – This app makes managing your time an easy proposition because it allows you set up a daily schedule of activities.
- Cruise Card Control – This app helps to make you aware of end of sail surprise expenses at the purser's desk. It helps you keep track of expenses.
- Skype – Depending on which phone you own, Skype allows you the freedom to instant message, make a phone call, and videoconference for free. This is a great app for keeping in touch with the family and can eliminate the need for expensive travel.

RV (Recreational Vehicle) Travel

In my previous book, *RVing & Your Retirement Lifestyle: A Cost Effective Way to Live Your Dreams* (*booklocker.com*), I discuss how the RV lifestyle is an accommodating and cost-effective way to realize your retirement dreams. You do indeed have a true sense of freedom and adventure.

Consider some of the frugal advantages: There is no need to purchase expensive airplane tickets, hotel accommodations, and a rental car when you arrive at your destination. And, you do not have to dine out each day because you can prepare all of your meals in the comfort of your RV. Remember, you travel with your own living room, kitchen, and bathroom. We have been RVing for forty years. Indeed, we have prepared some incredible gourmet meals in our coach.

Studies have been done to compare the costs of various types of vacations. PFK Consulting came up with the conclusion that a family of four (in case you are thinking of traveling with grandchildren), can spend up to 74% less when traveling in an RV.

In case you do not understand the nature of the RV, there are two types: motorized and non-motorized. The motorized type would include all categories of motorhomes while the non-motorized includes trailers that you tow behind a vehicle. Obviously, if you are interested in a trailer, you will need a vehicle that is capable of towing the unit. That would involve an SUV or truck or van with at least a six-cylinder engine.

If you think you'd like to try this form of travel consider renting an RV. Check out the Cruise America (*cruiseamerica.com*) website. This is a national rental company with locations in many states.

Another interesting frugal RV travel alternative is workamping. This involves working a few hours a day where you camp. Our National Park system offers campground host positions. In return for your work, you are offered free accommodations at the parks.

Some Budget Friendly Vacations

If you are on a tight budget, as most of us are these days, you may be thinking of giving up your vacation. We all know how good is to get a way for a while, particularly related to stress relief.

Here are some suggestions from AARP that you may have heretofore not thought about.

If you enjoy wandering through the woods, but are not so crazy about camping out, hut-to-hut hiking could be the answer. The Appalachian Mountain Club operates a network of back-country huts in the White Mountains of New Hampshire. Meals are served family style and sleeping is in coed bunkhouses from June to September.

How about visiting a national park? There are about 400 national parks to choose from, and you can customize your vacation a variety of ways. Accommodations range from remote camping to tent and RV sites to historic lodges. Make certain that you search the National Park Service (*nps.gov*) website.

Visit a Caribbean beach. If you focus on islands that have lots of all-inclusive packages that attract crowds, then the trip can be very frugal. Look for a volume discounter that offers airfare and lodging cost bundled. The savings can be dramatic.

CHAPTER 7: PERSONAL GROWTH & THE LEARNING PROCESS

In my first book, *The New Professional Person's Retirement Lifestyle*, I describe in detail the need for the retiree to create that all-important plan for retirement. It is crucial that you literally take stock of yourself in an effort to determine what you would really like to do in retirement. That plan should be long-term in nature, as we are living longer, healthier lives. And, you should do what you really want. Do not be afraid to experiment.

As I've previously indicated, if your plan focuses only on leisure activities, the costs can be enormous. So much for a frugal retirement lifestyle!

On the other hand, if you focus on personal development, costs can be inexpensive. The cost of learning can be quite reasonable. As retired teachers, my wife and I continue to focus on learning and growing. It makes us feel alive and healthy and keeps us mentally acute. Scientists have long acknowledged that keeping a brain active and stimulated is essential towards living a greatly increased lifespan. A commitment to lifelong learning helps to improve your memory and in general, improve your brainpower.

There are a variety of ways you can keep on learning and growing in a frugal fashion. Again, this process would allow you to live on less money than leisure-based retirement.

Here are some frugal suggestions for personal development.

Adult Education

Most local boards of education offer adult education courses. Those courses are extensive and costs are quite reasonable. Smaller communities may offer joint programs in conjunction with neighboring towns. And, courses are usually offered during the day or early evening. A sampling of courses available in my small town in Connecticut included the following:

- all aspects of financial planning
- all aspects of computer operations and associated software
- weaving
- creative writing
- auto repair
- ballroom dancing
- golf lessons
- tennis lessons
- Chinese cooking
- Italian cooking
- vegetarian cooking
- seamanship
- yoga
- CPR
- reading classic novels
- candle making
- foreign language basic conversation

Other Local Community Resources

Most towns and cities have a senior citizen center, a recreation center, and even a YMCA. Events are varied and reasonably priced. Senior centers can offer great deals on day trips to local attractions, day classes of general interest, and various types of sports lessons.

The local YMCA can be a wonderful resource. You can get a very precise idea about what is being offered if you log onto their website (*ymca.net*). There are around 2,400 branches around the country.

The Learning Process Never Ends
COLLEGE COURSEWORK

Most public colleges and universities will allow you to take courses without being enrolled. And, as a senior citizen, you may even be able to take courses for free, as a number of states offer tuition wavers to people 62 years of age or older. What a great way to explore a hidden passion that you have. You can check out the many high-quality institutions that offer free classes by simply searching a particular university or college. Although these courses will not lead to a college degree (if that is what you want), they are a good way to keep your mind alert.

DISTANCE LEARNING

If you'd rather not drive or are unable to drive to a campus to take courses, distance learning may be just the thing for you. It just may be that if you are over the age of 60, you may be a bit physically worn out. In addition, with the cost of traditional desktop computers and laptop computers becoming much more frugal (below $200), it is easier to afford Internet access. Online coursework does indeed make life a bit easier since you can take classes when you want to.

In case you are not familiar with the terminology, distance learning involves taking classes online. You can complete your coursework at home on your computer. Needless to say, you will need to be somewhat technology proficient. And, if you choose to do so, you can readily work towards a college degree.

The University of Phoenix (*uoponline.com*) offers a wide variety of degrees. And, there are actual campuses around the country if you choose not to take classes online. A good resource is Yahoo Distance Learning (*yahoo.com/education*).

By the way, if you have to pay for coursework, and you are not certain you can afford to do so based on your retirement income, there is another possibility.

There is financial aid available for senior citizens. Companies such as Calgon have set up special financial aid programs for senior citizens. As I indicated previously, many colleges also offer seniors special reduced tuition or audit programs. There are also organizations such as the Janet Rankin Foundation set up for this purpose.

I suggest that you log onto the Free Education (*free-ed.net*) and explore their free courses and programs. Most users of the site are participating in some sort of higher education. The site also has a link for grants. You may be qualified. The colleges at *free-ed.net* include Arts and Humanities, Technology, Allied Health, Social Sciences, Education, and College of Public Services.

Another great site for the frugal retiree is *openculture.com.* Their goal is to "bring together high quality cultural media for the worldwide lifelong learning community." The site lists over 375 free online courses from colleges and universities. You can refresh your math skills, study history, economics, marketing, and even quantum physics. You will find something for everyone at Open Culture. They offer free movies and audio books. There are podcasts available for law school or business school.

The Hewlett Packard Learning Center online offers many courses on a wide range of topics. Courses include computer programming, html, web design, and many other business related topics.

If you need assistance with learning about the tools of technology, then you should certainly explore SeniorNet (*seniornet.org*). Since 1986, they have helped over 1,000,000 people over the age of 50 gain knowledge through computers. That is, they have learned how computers and the Internet can enhance their lives and enable them to share their knowledge and wisdom with the world. And, the cost to join is frugal. The membership is only $40 for the first year.

SeniorNet offers two choices for a learning environment. First, you can join one of their many learning centers around the country and take advantage of the many computer courses. At my local learning center in Arizona they are offering workshops on e-mail fundamentals, file management fundamentals, and shopping and travel planning on the Internet. Second, you can join their online learning centers. Online they offer 300 senior friendly lessons on Microsoft Word, Excel, PowerPoint, Vista, and Adobe Photoshop, and more. At the time of this writing you could enroll in the Online Learning Center for only $99 per year, which allows you access to those 300 lessons for a year. Log onto their website to examine the plethora of opportunities that are available.

LEARN A LANGUAGE ONLINE

There are a variety of websites that you can log onto if you are interested in learning a new language.

Word2word.com offers links to online courses in most languages. The best part here is that most of the links offer free tutorials. *Spanishromance.com* also provides resources to learn Spanish for free. Learn Chinese (*learn-chinese-language-online.com)* features information to help you learn Chinese with topics including speaking, writing, grammar, and proficiency testing

VISIT MUSEUMS ONLINE AND TAKE A VIRTUAL TOUR

Here's a great intellectually stimulating frugal idea: Visit a museum via your computer. Many museums offer an interesting online presence through their respective links. Ultimately, you can pull together a vast array of exhibits and collections including classic art and architecture.

The Museum of Online Museums (*coudal.com/moom.php*) offers many links to brick-and-mortar museums. Most of these sites will present multiple exhibits from their collections. There really is something for everybody at this site including the Smithsonian Art Museum, a link of Russian museums, art treasures from Kyoto, the Van Gogh Gallery, even a skateboard museum.

VLMP (Virtual Library Museum Pages) (*archives.icom.museum/vlmp/*) is a worldwide directory of online museums that are organized by country.

MuseumStuff.com, or commonly known as Museums of the World, boasts a staggering variety of educational links accompanied by a large amount of interactive virtual exhibits with links to dozens of museum shops. Most of their links are topically arranged.

ELDERHOSTEL (*roadscholar.org*)

Road Scholar is a non-profit program offered by Elderhostel that inspires adults to learn, discover and travel. Their learning adventures utilize expert instructors and stimulate friendship.

Their adventures take place by train, in national parks, and many are inter-generational by nature.

At the time of this writing, they offer more than 7,000 educational adventures in 150 countries. They include comfortable accommodations along with excellent values. You can experience cultural excursions and study cruises to walking, biking, independent city discoveries, art history, music and dance, science and nature, philosophy, and much more.

At the website you can easily search a program by location, interest, activity level, and by most any category.

Recent tours included cultural studies in Morocco, exploration and studies at Mt. Rushmore, and a cruise study from Boston to Montreal.

The website also features a special offer link where programs are presented with reduced prices, or with airfare included.

ONLINE LIBRARY ACCESS

Online library resources offer a wealth of information. Three of the most of commonly performed tasks are:

- checking on book or audio availability
- reserving books
- renewing books

You can also do the following tasks on a frugal basis:

- Read scholarly journals.
- Read newspapers and search through newspaper archives.
- Visit the online reference desk and learn about areas such as genealogy, history, geography, government, music, and business.
- Search databases of libraries online including government libraries, law libraries, public libraries, and medical libraries.

Audio Resources

Another way to promote personal growth on a frugal level is with audio programs. There are a variety of websites that offer free or reasonably priced downloads. One of those sources is iTunes (*itunes.com*). Of course, you will need to open an account. You can download books for under $10 to your iPhone, iPad, or iPod touch. A large variety of reference books are available.

Be certain to go to *Education-Portal.com*, which lists 50 free places to find both fiction and nonfiction ebooks, audio books, poetry, and reference books. At the time of this writing there were at least 15 sources listed for free audio books.

Learn Out Loud (*learnoutloud.com*) offers 3,000 free audio titles, including books, lectures, sermons, interviews, and other resources.

CHAPTER 8: CULTURAL ACTIVITIES & THE FINE ARTS

If you enjoy cultural activities, specifically the fine arts, there are a variety of frugal choices available to you.

Fine arts typically include the visual arts and performing art forms such as painting, sculpture, music, dance, theatre, photography, and even certain aspects of electronic media (video, digital photography, and digital printmaking).

Aside from the traditional ways to enjoying these activities, such as enrolling in private classes or taking a college course, there may be other alternatives.

Theater

You may be able to participate in day trips sponsored by the local senior center or parks and recreation department. My research has shown that the cost of these trips is generally quite reasonable since these organizations are non-profit.

In addition, check out performances by my local colleges, universities, and theatre groups. My wife and I regularly obtain senior citizen discounts.

Another resourceful way to attend theatrical events is to volunteer at the production. For example, as an usher your responsibilities include escorting patrons to their seats and your reward is usually a free seat.

There are also discount online merchants that sell tickets at great prices if you can book at the last minute. One of our favorites is *showuptickets.com,* which I discuss later.

Another very frugal strategy to employ, if you have the flexibility, is to obtain theatre tickets at the last minute. My wife and I frequently attend shows by arriving at the theatre one hour before production time. At that point, tickets are reduced by 50%. Certainly, you will need to check with your local box office to see if they do something similar. In the long run, these savings can be substantial. By the way, you may find that purchasing theatre tickets may be less expensive if you do so directly from the box office as opposed to using an agency such as Ticketmaster, which charges additional fees.

Museums

Museums are a great source of cultural activities. In addition to ongoing exhibit changes, most museums offer a calendar of events. Many offer lifelong learning seminars, lectures, and trips of a cultural nature at a reduced rate for seniors. You may also find concerts, poetry readings and other classes. Be certain to check the offering at your local museum.

Seasonal Events

When the weather outside is reasonable, and you are looking for entertainment, log onto to your town or city website to see what is going on. You can also check the website of the nearest orchestra.

During the summer months, there may be a variety of concerts available for your enjoyment. The city of New Haven, CT offers a variety of concerts, especially during its annual Festival of Arts and Ideas. Recently, we attended a concert and lecture by Yo-Yo Ma, all free of charge.

Many cities and towns also offer free or low-cost concerts at parks, museums, and local theatre venues. Summer jazz concerts are offered as part of a summer series in many locations. The City of Scottsdale, Arizona offers a series of outdoor concerts beginning in January on most Sunday afternoons. We attend many of those free-of-charge events that present a wide variety of music.

New York's free Shakespeare in the Park is very well known, albeit tickets may be difficult to obtain. Check your local newspaper's event calendar to see what events are offered. You can also Google your town or city's name to see if any seasonal film series of other events are being offered.

Art

One of my favorite all-inclusive websites for retirement in general has always been AARP (*aarp.org*). Most of the suggestions presented are creative, expressive, and in general, ideas that will no doubt enhance your retirement. And, they are frugal as well.

If you have ever had the desire to discover your inner artist, then look into their very creative way to draw and paint.

At the time of this writing they are offering a free online course with Steve Aimone, author of a popular art book.

The course includes drawing exercises, a game, instructional videos, and a variety of materials to inspire you to pursue your art.

At this point, there are 750 members of this artistic community that have uploaded nearly 800 drawings. This allows your virtual classmates to examine and thoughtfully critique your work. A great feature of this program is that it allows you to take these virtual classes at any time in an effort to devote as much time as much time as you would like.

Examples of the curriculum include shapes, art appreciation, doodling, drawing your inner self, color exploration, and how to use a grid.

In addition, the AARP Art Group Directory offers a plethora of posts at the time of this writing relating to "expressive drawing and creativity." The discussions involve keeping art alive in our lives. Recent discussions include drawing prompts and various drawing exercises.

Do not forget to check into local art courses offered by your town or city park and recreation, senior center, and adult education departments. Courses are varied and will usually meet the needs of all participants. My wife is currently enrolled in an oil-painting course through our recreation department at a total cost of only $40 dollars for 6 weeks. She feels very good about her progress and very much enjoys the class. I particularly enjoy her feeling of satisfaction and the frugal cost.

"ARTSY" ACTIVITIES

Then there are economical arts and crafts activities that are a way for us retirees to keep both their minds and hands active. The resulting projects can be useful as gifts or decorations.

Here are some suggestions:

- Clay projects - Molding clay can be rolled into items such as vases and bowls. You can also use play-dough.
- Mosaics – Very similar to a puzzle design.
- sewing and knitting – These projects can be adapted according to your abilities. Obviously, you will need to have reasonably good eyesight.
- Photography – Photos are a great source of creativity, especially in this age of technology. Aside from traditional scrapbooking, there are digital scrapbooking and slideshows that can easily be shared with various family members. If you can work on your computer, there are even possibilities for calendars and greeting cards.
- Sculpture – If you are somewhat resourceful, you can sculpt plastic material, stone, metal, or wood. Sculptures

can be created by carving, assembling, welding, and molding.

- Calligraphy – This art form is often called the art of fancy lettering. Forms can include hand-lettered inscriptions and designs to fine-art pieces. Many local town recreation departments offer courses in calligraphy.
- Film – Filmmaking is still popular in the area of fine arts. Obviously, the technology has changed dramatically over the years. If you are interested in filmmaking, there are a variety of websites that can be of great help.

Music

If you have a musical background, as my wife and I do, you can certainly have frugal fun with your talents. We have been playing together for 40 years in a variety of ways. We've performed in nightclubs and musical variety shows and musicals. Nowadays, we accompany some singers. On most occasions we use our combined talents to play music at nursing homes and assisted living facilities. This is a great venue for giving back, and residents have a great time when we perform. So, if you have any musical talents, why not "keep on playing!" If you know other retirees with musical talents, contact them and see if they are interested.

A large number of community organizations exist around the country such as musical theatre, choirs, and orchestras that seek out participants with no particular requirements. Many of these groups charge no fees and do not require auditions.

The benefits of participating in these activities are varied. Certainly one of the most prominent is the extension of the quality of life. You are increasing your physical activity along with improving self-esteem. Many physicians feel that music does all of this. In some sense, "music may be an alterative to medicine." So says Dr. Walter Nieri, a geriatrician who is director of the Banner Sun Health Research Center for Healthy Aging. Although there may be no scientific studies to show that it extends life it does make people live better. It may even help them live longer.

The Sun City Arizona Concert Band has around 100 players with no auditions required. Attendance is so good they have to turn people away. Members include an 82-year-old trumpet player and an 80-year-old saxophone player.

CHAPTER 9: YOU CAN STILL WORK!

Over the course of my last four books, I've interviewed a plethora of retirees in regards to that all-important plan for the future. I can tell you most assuredly that many of us desire to continue working.

If you feel that way, for whatever the reason, there is absolutely nothing wrong with that. You want to be happy and feel a sense of inner satisfaction. For many of us, that may involve working.

A major reason for working is to experience a sense of reinvention. Perhaps you would like to experience a new vocation that you've dreamt about. You may also have an innate desire to continue to be productive and stay mentally and physically active. This new work may indeed lead you down a path of happiness.

Given the theme of this book, the most significant reason for you to work may simply be economic. That is, you would like to pay your bills and have some fun, too. Or, perhaps you simply need help paying those bills and would like to increase the size of your nest egg. The extra money will help compensate you for the income lost after leaving the workforce as well as help you make the adjustment to retirement. In fact, a bridge job may subjectively help to contribute to your well-being.

You may be among the older Americans that are concerned about supporting their retirement needs. According to a recent AARP survey, 61% of respondents interviewed indicated that their savings had decreased since the start of the recession. Furthermore, the number of people over the age of 55 has risen by 12% as well.

The U.S. Bureau of Labor Statistics indicates that more people over the age of 55 are working than ever before. Many people, even past the age of 75, are rejoining the workforce.

According to a recent Employee Benefit Research Institute (EBRI) survey, 72% of Americans polled indicate that they plan to supplement their income by working. The reasons for this may include:

- the lack of availability of traditional pension plans (the shift has been to 401(k) plans that rely on workers to set aside money and invest wisely)
- insufficient retirement savings (which certainly became more difficult to achieve during the recession)
- rising healthcare costs
- the recent economic downturn
- increasing life spans

Certainly there are certain considerations for you to make such as being able to draw a pension and salary from the same employer if that is the scenario. You would also want to be certain that there are no conflicts with your Social Security benefits.

I'd like to present some suggestions for working during retirement with the goal in mind of supplementing your income. Again, you will need to put these ideas in perspective based on your individual needs. Hopefully, if you decide to continue working, you will be lucky enough to find a job. At the time of this writing, there are more older people who want jobs than there are jobs available. The unemployment rate for people over 55 has doubled from 2007 to 2011.

If you are desirous of returning to work in an effort to be able to fulfill your retirement dreams financially, there are some variables for you to consider. For example, would you prefer to work indoors or outdoors? Can you work with others or would you rather work alone? How important is the amount of money you would receive (consider whether the job is worthwhile monetarily)? How well do you deal with stress at this point in your life? How about being creative? Try something you've always dreamed about doing.

Temporary Work

Temporary work can encompass a wide range of skills. Jobs many include dishwashing, keyboarding, and working on a loading dock.

If you possess highly specialized skills there may be other more lucrative opportunities available. If this is the case, you will need to locate the right agency to serve your needs. Check websites such as *kforce.com, kelleyservices.com*, and *manpower.com.* Kelley has instituted a special program to place older adults. You can also contact temporary agencies located in your town or city. Be certain to inquire what positions the agency specializes in. Some deal with technical placements while others deal with positions such as butlers, drivers, housekeepers, chefs, and so on. It is important to understand that the temp agency will take a percentage of your wages, usually for as long as you work at their placement.

Try to network with people who have a similar background to yours and see if any companies are looking for temporary employees with your experience. If so, then submit your resume to these companies.

Be certain to update your resume whenever you complete a temporary work assignment. The extra experience may help you find additional work as a temporary employee.

If you envision temporary work as a regular happening during retirement, then consider updating your skills by taking classes at a local community college or online.

Part-Time Work

Part-time work works perfectly if you have a busy schedule, need a little extra income, and want to have fun doing something different.

In a recent article at their website, AARP has come up with 5 part-time jobs for retirees.

1. Blogger - Obviously computer skills in this area are a must. A successful blog must encompass subject matter that is valuable to people who are interested in your topic. AARP suggests that you begin by logging onto *problogger.net*.

2. Athletic Coach/Umpire/Referee – Check into a coach, referee, umpire or scorekeeper position at your local high schools.

3. Teacher's Aide – Basically, if you have nerves of steel and a great deal of patience, the rewards can be plentiful. Duties of a teacher's aide can include grading papers, recording grades, data entry, and setting up equipment. You may also be assigned cafeteria or hall duty.

4. Tour Jobs – These jobs can be very attractive if you are a history buff and can indeed remember dates and facts. You will also need to possess good people interaction skills. Depending on the job you may have to be on your feet for many hours at a time.

5. Convention Center jobs – These jobs can be a good source for part-time jobs with a variety of skill requirements. There may be food service opportunities, parking lot attendants, parking lot cashiers, ushers, and booth attendant jobs available in this area. Check out *convention.net*.

Bridge Employment

No, this type of work does not involve road construction! Basically, bridge employment is defined as a job that one works after leaving a full-time career. The intention is to gradually withdraw over time from the full-time labor force participation. The process can be viewed as a transition into retirement. Bridge jobs can entail many of the previously discussed characteristics of part-time and temporary work.

Bridge jobs can help the retiree feel fulfilled and productive and at the same time allow for a feeling of connectivity to the outside world.

I think it is important to note that unless you are looking to reinvent yourself with a lifelong passion, a bridge job can be a source of pressure and stress that can make the adjustment to retirement more difficult.

Care take Someone Else's Property

These days, in a continuing effort to make ends meet during retirement, more retirees are working taking care of other people's property. This is a great way to temporarily supplement your income. Many property owners prefer retired people because of an associated maturity level that equates with common sense and reliability.

Check out the Caretaker Gazette (*caretaker.org*). This newsletter contains openings for house sitting jobs. Oftentimes, homeowners need sitters while on an extended vacation or a corporate retreat. Positions may be available at estates, mansions, farms, ranches, resort homes, camps, hunting and fishing lodges, and even private islands. In addition, many national parks are in need of groundskeepers during the winter months.

Substitute Teaching

During the 33 years that I was a public school teacher, one of my responsibilities was the securing of substitute teachers at my school. The task was a formidable one, to say the least.

It will always be a challenge to attract reliable and capable people. Although the compensation may not be high, the accompanying responsibilities are limited. You simply follow the directions and lesson plans left by the regular teaching staff. I've always perceived substitute teaching as a way to give back and perform a great service for the school district. There continues to be a shortage of substitutes in most districts.

If you have specialized skills, your services are in even greater demand. You do not need to be a certified teacher to substitute.

If you were a teacher in your former life, your services are greatly needed. I have a personal friend who was a teacher for 35 years and substitute teaches when he can. He is very happy doing so. Obviously, this is an income-enhancing activity with a great deal of flexibility.

If you think you are interested, simply contact the personnel office of your local Board of Education. In addition, you can do a search on Google by simply typing in "substitute teacher jobs." By doing so, a plethora of information will be available to you.

Working for a Nonprofit

My wife and I have spent many years volunteering for a nonprofit. If you work for a nonprofit in retirement, you can make some extra cash as well as embrace a call to help out the organization give back to society. This should make the experience rewarding. Although the salary may not be high, it will certainly help your financial perspective.

There are more than 1.5 million nonprofits in this country. Those include charities, foundations, private schools, community colleges, churches, and trade associations.

AARP suggests that consider the following if you are interested:

- What issues do you really care about?
- What skills do you have to offer?
- Consider taking a course to add to your skills.
- Research the nonprofit you are interested in.

They also suggest the following examples of the types of nonprofit jobs that are available:

- Administrative Assistant
- Volunteer Manager – A main responsibility here would be the recruiting of volunteers.
- Marketing/Communications Manager – Duties would include drafting press releases, involvement with social media, and email correspondence.
- Recreational Therapist – As the population ages, there is a growing demand for people who can artistically provide activities for older adults.
- Fundraiser – Obviously, you would need to be good at asking for money from donors. You would also need good listening skills.

Check out websites including *idealist.org, change.org,* Bridgestar, and *encore.org* and Linkedin.

Working in a Retirement Community

As an extension of the discussion of living in a retirement community in the chapter on "Home and Transportation" in this book, I'd like to present some thoughts in regards to working in such a community.

You may consider retirement locales as sources of opportunities to find work. If you are located in or thinking of purchasing a home in a community that offers a variety of amenities, there may be work available. There is a normal need for personnel to provide products and services to the population beyond the permanent labor force that maintains the facility. Other residents may need your services as well.

The following positions can illustrate some of the jobs within a retirement community. Most often, there are bulletin boards within the specific community that features job opening:

- telephone operators
- bookkeepers and accountants
- hosts in the dining rooms
- beauticians and hare care personnel
- financial and tax advice
- sales
- receptionists
- maintenance
- security

If you are interested in finding work in a new community or one that is about to be developed, this could be an opportunity for you to begin a start-up business. There will be many products and services that new arrivals to the retirement community will desire. Here are some examples:

- interior decorator
- technology specialist
- landscaping specialist
- nutritionist
- airport limousine service
- photographer
- relocation specialist

The authors of *Reworking Retirement* suggest the following steps upon arriving at a retirement community if you have something to sell or market:

1. Set up a website.
2. Print business cards.
3. Get a copy of the community directory.
4. Place a classified ad.
5. Sponsor a local event.
6. Run a seminar of give a free lecture on a topic.
7. Network.

Working From Home

Working from home is a great idea if you are looking to save money and time. Indeed, it does make a great deal of sense if you have difficulty getting around for lack of transportation or physical issues. Given the changes in the employment landscape in recent years, this is a viable alternative. Obviously, you will need to have some technology skills and be comfortable with talking on the telephone.

AARP suggests the following five great work-at-home jobs for retirees:

CUSTOMER SERVICE REPRESENTATIVE

You will definitely need an up-to-date computer, a high-speed Internet connection, and probably a dedicated landline for work use.

Basically, you are answering incoming calls, taking orders, tracking existing orders, troubleshooting, and provide technical support.

Potential employers can include Hilton Hotels, American Airlines, and 1-800-Flowers.

ONLINE JUROR

Certain online companies will pay you to sit on mock juries to give attorneys and other jury consultants feedback on cases they are working on. You may have to listen to audio and view video presentations, along with reading various documents. Companies such as *ejury.com* and *onlineverdict.com* are examples.

VIRTUAL ASSISTANT

Duties for this job involve sending out letters, making travel arrangements and basically assisting with administrative tasks. Check out *ivaa.org* and *virtualassistantjobs.com.*

ONLINE TUTOR

The subjects most in demand in this area are history, physics, science, and math. Examples of employers are *tutor.com* and *kaplankids.com.*

WRITER/EDITOR

Although you do not need to be a professional, you will need a clear understanding of sentence and paragraph construction, spelling, grammar, and punctuation. Jobs can include copyediting and proofreading. *Careerbuilding.com* offers a wide range of postings.

Here are some additional work-at-home sites to check out:

AlpineAccess.com – virtual call center using home-based customer service agents

arise.com – answer calls, e-mail and chat requests for global companies

careers.convergysworkathome.com – customer care agents at home *intellicare.com* – call center that provides clinical and non-clinical telephone services to healthcare providers

onlineverdict.com – provides online case reviews and juror feedback services to attorneys

workingsolutions.com – offering home-based customer service agent positions

2020research.com – market research services for professional marketing researchers

Second Career Jobs

If you do decide to return to the workforce, AARP has come with a list of jobs that are the fastest growing at the time of this writing. They feel that these jobs may be particularly appropriate for workers over the age of 50. Some of the suggestions include:

- home health aide: 460,000 new jobs projected by 2018
- personal and home care aide
- medical assistant
- dental assistant: 62,000 jobs by 2018
- physical therapist assistant or aide
- financial examiner: average pay is $70,000
- floral designer
- loan officer
- retail salesperson
- administrative assistant
- building maintenance

Suggestions for Locations to Launch a New Career in Retirement

As previously mentioned, many senior retirees are continuing to work past the age of 65, both for the money and because they enjoy working. They may have come to terms with the need to develop that all-important plan for retirement, which includes reinventing oneself.

If you are considering relocating, an important consideration is the unemployment rate. If you are in a town with a vibrant economy, you may have an easier time finding work than those locations with fewer job opportunities. Be certain to check the job opportunities in the area that you would like to relocate to.

In a recent article, U. S. News looked for locales with below-average unemployment and a solid record of new job creation over the past decade. They also considered a reasonable cost of living, access to healthcare facilities, and outdoor and recreational opportunities. Cities with a large number of government jobs may be somewhat immune to the current economic downturn. Typically, those cites would include many of the state capitals.

Retirees may also want to consider looking for work in locations with major healthcare facilities, especially if they have a background in any of the healthcare or social assistance. Nurses, home health aides, and medical assistants are expected to be among the fastest growing jobs.

Check out the following ten great places to reinvent your work experience during retirement:

- Ames, IA
- Harrisonburg, VA
- Lincoln, NE
- Lubbock, TX
- Madison, WI
- Manhattan, KS
- Oklahoma City, OK
- Richland, WA
- Rochester, MN
- State College, PA

Earn Money From Your Hobbies

Here is an interesting idea: Turn your favorite pastime into a source of income. The website *about.com* has come up with the following suggestions:

ART AND CRAFTS

How about teaching art classes either privately or at craft store? Perhaps you can sell your work at craft shows or art galleries.

PHOTOGRAPHY

Do you have a special talent as a photographer? You may be able to sell your photos online, or get freelance work at a newspaper or even do wedding and event photography and videography.

SPORTS

Have you ever thought about being an umpire, referee, or coach? You may even be able to become a personal trainer. Or, how about a scorekeeper or statistician?

ANIMAL CARE

If you love animals, you could obtain work as dog walker, pet-sitter, or even as a groomer.

MUSIC

As I previously mentioned, my wife and I are long-time musicians. Our experiences include musical direction, accompanying, and participating in a variety of musical organizations and productions. If you have a particular talent, you may even be able to give private lessons.

COOKING
Possible jobs in this area include teaching cooking classes, catering, or selling your foods at farmer's markets.

GARDENING
If gardening is a hobby of yours, you could hire yourself out as a gardener or landscaper or sell your produce at a local farmer's market.

FITNESS
If you are physically fit, you could be a lifeguard, personal trainer, a teacher in an exercise class, or even a river guide.

Organizations
SeniorJobBank.org – This is a non-profit that is solely devoted to bringing together employers with qualified older job seekers. The jobs are listed by state. So, for example, when I searched the New Haven, CT ZIP code, I came up with around 11,000 job openings. The jobs are listed both on a part-time and full-time basis.

RetirementJobs.com – This site caters to seniors. They appreciate the intrinsic values of older workers including dependability, a strong work ethic, and flexibility of work schedule, and pay. The employment service is free for job seekers. Prospective employers post open positions to the site. The job search link at the website allows you to specify your part-time preference and both the nature of the work you are interested in the distance from your ZIP code

Workforce50.com – This organization attempts to bring diverse employment opportunities to the over-50 population. In addition to their search mechanism, the site offers a variety of trade resources, job search resources, suggestions for marketing yourself, and even a home-based business toolkit.

Seniors4hire.org – This is an online community for people over 50 and companies that are looking to recruit them. Membership is free and you are allowed to post your resume and post job wanted notifications.

experienceworks.org – The goal of ExperienceWorks is to assist older adults get the training they need to find good jobs in their communities. They attempt to improve the lives of older people through community service and employment. A major emphasis is to help people who are low income.

craigslist.org – Craigslist provides jobs listing to more than 100 community sites in the U.S. Jobs are posted alphabetically and updated every day. When I clicked on the part-time link in the Hartford, CT area at the time of this writing, there were 1,000 postings. You will need to sort through these postings carefully.

encore.org – This site connects people over 50 to post-retirement jobs with social purpose, mainly in education, government, and the nonprofit sectors.

retiredbrains.com – Employers featured here are looking for seasoned staff.

grayhairmanagement.com – This organization specializes in helping executives and senior managers find part-time and contract work.

comingofage.org – A variety of resources are offered here for people over 50 as well as listings of government jobs and nonprofits.

aarp.org/work – Among the variety of very useful links offered at the site are working after retirement. The site is regularly updated with current information.

ssa.gov/retire2 – Social Security information offered regarding working while receive Social Security benefits

dinosaur-exchange.com – Lists employment opportunities around the world

ebay.com – Become a vendor on eBay and make money selling all kinds of things.

CHAPTER 10: HOME AND TRANSPORTATION

As I've mentioned previously in this book (and in all of my four other books), it is so very important that you create a plan for retirement that you will definitely follow. The reason for this is simple: You need to have certain things in place. If you have set goals for yourself that lead to a different lifestyle and hence may require a certain financial status, will you have the money when you need it? Will you be financially independent?

Related to this independence are issues that arise when thinking about your ideal living situation. The primary consideration for many is whether you can remain in your current home due to financial and or physical challenges. (You will find further discussion on this topic in the chapter on Frugal Relocation in this book). Questions to ask yourself include:

- Can I actually afford my current location? You may want to consider a region that would help you make ends meet financially. Perhaps a lower cost of living can be found elsewhere or you may even be able to pool resources with others as a way to cut costs. This will allow more cash to be available for your intended retirement lifestyle.
- Do I want to spend less time and money on household chores and maintenance? A homeowners association bears the cost of most external repairs on a condominium. Remember, a condo translates to no property to maintain.

- Is my environment generally supportive for retirement and aging?

Keep in mind that your retirement needs changes over time. That is, what is important early on may not be so as you age. When we bought our second residence in Arizona, we never thought about being able to negotiate stairs in later years. So, if you are healthy enough to be very active at one point during your retirement, which may not be the case as the years progress.

Downsizing: Buying Versus Renting

One of the most common ways that retirees gain some financial independence is downsizing. If you (and your spouse) are living in a 4,000-square foot house, perhaps you should consider downsizing. This course of action becomes even more pronounced if you are retired and are struggling to make ends meet. Then there is the decision as to whether it is better to own or rent. These days, since real estate values have fallen so precipitously, it is a difficult decision.

If you purchased your home 40 years ago, as I did, and you paid a reasonable price for the property, it may make perfect sense to keep it. As long as your expenses are under control and you are comfortable with the size and location of your home, you may be fine. If, however, there are two of you residing in a large estate type of setting, you may want to consider selling or renting the property. Much of this decision depends on whether your financial condition is limiting the achievement of the goals you've set for retirement. It may be important for you to consider the current and future value of your home. For example, at the peak of the housing boom in 2006, your home may have been worth $300,000. Perhaps it is now worth only $200,000. It could take 10 to 12 years for your house to return to that value. Can you wait that long or do you need to sell now? Many financial experts suggest that you may be better off staying in your current home, due to the fact that buying and selling a home can incur fees and charges that can take years to recover from. It is certainly very much a personal decision.

Daniel Solin, author of *The Smartest Money Book You'll Ever Read,* suggests you consider the following factors when deciding whether to buy or rent:

- price to rent ratio – This is the ratio of the price of a home to the annual rent of an equivalent home. The higher the ratio, that is, the higher the purchase price is relative to the rent, the more it makes sense to rent.
- cost of owning versus renting – In addition to what I've previously discussed, Solin feels that you need to consider your home as an investment and it should hopefully match the returns of a balanced portfolio.

If you have the capability, many financial experts suggest paying off your mortgage, especially if your balance is a moderate one. Doing so can cut your living expenses in retirement if you suddenly need money or there is a change in your housing plans. Full ownership can be a hedge against extreme economic risks, such as hyperinflation. In addition, if you are burdened by mortgage payments, refinancing with a new 30-year loan can help, regardless of your age.

Another alternative to think about is to create a new living situation with friends or family. With a number of people sharing expenses, it may be more accommodating to your financial capabilities. Needless to say, if you do this, be certain that these are people that you can live with. See my discussion on cohousing later in this chapter.

As a more extreme measure, if you cannot afford the house you are living in and are unable to sell it for enough to pay the mortgage, you can walk away and rent. It does not make financial sense to exhaust your retirement savings in a futile effort to hold on. Of course, you can discuss these options with a bankruptcy attorney. The most important consideration here is to be able to implement and enjoy the plan for retirement that you have created.

Chris Farrell, author of the book, *The New Frugality*, suggests the following guidelines when comparing owning versus renting your home:

- Compare the cost of owning versus renting. Depending on the numbers, either one may good for your situation.
- Buy only if the deal is financially conservative. (This is especially relevant given the current nature of the economy).
- Keep the financing simple.
- Smaller is both financially smart and socially sustainable. Home ownership can be potentially disastrous for people who stretch their finances.

The author feels that crunching the "rent versus own" numbers help to keep your emotions in check. If you purchase a home, especially during the current down turned economy, you hope that home prices will rise. This will certainly help to justify the purchase price. He also suggests that smaller is beautiful—and I agree. I am still living in my original 1,500-square-foot house. The insurance, heating, and cooling costs are less, as are the taxes.

Then there is information presented in a recent article at the U.S. News & World Report Money website. They offer three reasons to rent in retirement, as opposed to owning.

1. Your home is a lousy investment. As there seems to be no end in sight for the negative downward trend in single family and condominium values, the equity you have in your home may disappear. If you are fortunate,

the value of your home may remain stagnant. Either way, they feel that your home equity could be put to better use.

2. Home maintenance is expensive and time consuming. Experienced homeowners may be fed up with yard work and various home related repairs, especially during our retirement years. Renting eliminates the money that is wasted on problems that are inherent to home ownership. Also, some utility costs may decline.

   I can attest to the dramatic difference in the amount of work and money that I spend on my home versus my condominium. Even though I own the condo, the homeowners association takes responsibility for most repairs and maintenance, so I am free to do other things. By the way, another great idea in an effort to live rent-free and save money is to become an apartment manager. If you can handle the responsibilities of being a manager, this could be a good option.

3. Home ownership ties you down. If you rent and become tired of where you are living, you do not have to go through the trouble and expense of selling. If you'd like to be closer to your children, you simply do not renew the lease.

What is the right size home for you?
Everyone experiences different living circumstances. You may need to look at your living situation in a new way. The process of determining the right size home for you involves carefully analyzing the space in your current home and how you utilize that space. You really want to best serve your needs and as I previously indicated, your new lifestyle.

There are a variety of personal considerations to think about if you are deciding whether to stay or leave your current home:

- Are you lonely?
- Do you feel unsafe where you currently reside? (This is also a key consideration when considering relocation.)
- Are you bored? Perhaps you are enjoying a busy retirement with a big social network and lots of activities. Maybe all you need is to move to a smaller more efficient home in a better location.
- Are you having difficulty accessing the rooms in your current home due to either a steep slope or stairs?
- As indicated previously, are you living in an older home that will require considerable repairs, such as roofing, flooring, plumbing, or wiring? Can you afford current and upcoming expenses? Going along with this thought, do you have a large yard that requires ongoing maintenance expenses?

If downsizing is in the future for you, it is certainly one of the most significant ways to live well on less. If indeed you do sell your current home, you may be able to pump up your nest egg with the proceeds of the sale and you are most likely going to spend less on maintenance, utilities, and property taxes year after year.

For example, the Hydes retired in 2008 just as the bear market was gaining steam. But because they cut the costs of keeping up a home from around $20,000 a year to $5,400 a year by trading down, the hit their portfolio took did not change their lifestyle. They sold their 5,000-square-foot home and bought a one-bedroom apartment. A $1,500 annual condo fee replaced the $7,000 they spent every year to keep up the yard and pool. Their property taxes fell by 72%, and utilities are a fraction of what they were. This couple now travels and dines out more frequently as well.

Here are some questions for you to consider:
- Do you really need all the space in your house?
- Are there rooms in your home that primarily serve as storage areas? Can they be put to better use such as an office or studio?
- Do you really need that guest room? We use our guest room in our Arizona home perhaps once a year.
- Think about future family needs. Do you expect to have children or other family returning home?

Three Ways to Save on Home Costs

Money Magazine suggests three ways to save on home expenses:

1. Negotiate on repairs and upkeep – Many contractors are facing a slumping market and will strike a deal to get your business. Many contractors say that they will negotiate labor costs and will drop prices by more than 10%. The same applies for house cleaners and landscapers. Be certain to obtain multiple quotes and try to be flexible about the timing of the job.

2. Trim the cost of borrowing – If you still have a mortgage, check to see if the rates have declined. If so, refinancing may be a possibility. You can negotiate lender fees. You may be able to lower your rate through a no-cost refinance. With this scenario, you will begin saving money right away. One of the most cost-effective things to do is to refinance from a thirty-year mortgage to a fifteen-year mortgage. Or, if you cannot handle the payments on a fifteen-year mortgage, consider a twenty-year mortgage. Either way, you will cut your interest rate and pay off the mortgage sooner. Be sure to check the value of your home before you refinance.

3. Get a deal on furniture – Higher shipping and materials costs are pushing furniture prices up. When sales during the

summer are slow, many smaller shops will make deals to move inventory. Ask for 20% off and do not settle for less than 10%. Gently-used floor models can go for 25% off. Sign-up for e-mails from furniture shopping sites.

Cohousing

An article from a recent AARP Bulletin presents some interesting alternatives to consider for retirement living.

These days many retirees would like to part of a community that shares common interests, values or resources. They would like to live where neighbors care about one another. Here are some suggestions:

Live with others who share similar lifestyles, backgrounds, and interests in a niche community. There are around 100 across the country. Prices and services vary, with some communities including meals, housekeeping, and social activities. It has been suggested that an individual household can save as much as $70,000 in a low-market, 20-unit cohousing community and $337,000 in a high-market project. For more information visit the AARP (*aarp.org/elderhousing*) site.

There are also around 100 cohousing units around the country where residents share some common space. Residents living in these communities care about each other and often form deep relationships. The biggest attraction is that residents are in complete control. They make their own rules and reach decisions by consensus. They may decide to cook a communal meal or weed a shared garden themselves. Usually you can join a cohousing project at any stage, including after the project is completed.

It is probably a good idea to join a project at an early stage so you can have more input in planning. For example, you may really want the site to be within walking distance of public transportation, restaurants, a library, a farmers market, and a community center. Hence, you would be driving less.

Log onto the Cohousing Company (*cohousingco.com*) website to see some examples of senior cohousing communities. This company emphasizes the sustainability aspect of cohousing as a natural way to preserve resources.

The Village Model is a concept where you live in your own home or apartment and receive discounted, vetted services and social opportunities. There are about 56 of these residences around the country at the time of this writing. The expectation is that these models will become more popular in the future because studies indicate that older people want to age in place.

Please check the AARP website above for the most up-to-date information regarding these living alternatives.

Home Sharing

Home sharing in retirement has become an increasingly popular alternative these days given the fluctuations in our economy. Organizations, both nonprofit and for profit, are popping up all over the United States with the goal of matching people for home sharing. For someone who lives on a fixed income and has a limited financial portfolio, even a small rental income can enhance financial security. Studies have shown that home sharing situations have readily progressed into a satisfying social environment of friends and relationships. This has led to good feelings about living and aging and added an element of excitement to retirement.

Basically, this is a long-term living arrangement in which unrelated residents live in a shared house, apartment, condominium, or mobile home.

It is important to understand that home sharing involves sharing a residence that may not be situated in a specific community. This residence can be a rental property for all residents or one of the residents can be the property owner.

This course of action has much appeal to retirees who are single and senior citizens in general and is a frugal way to live. It affords individuals a mix of privacy, socialization, and companionship. Residents share common areas of the home and experience a sense of community. In addition, studies have found that home share roommates complement each other's interests. Going to the gym together, traveling, and volunteering can be communal activities.

Home sharing can be a great option if you live alone and could benefit from the extra income that would reduce housing costs.

Certainly there are a great-deal of challenges that come with this type of living situation. Those include sharing responsibilities for housework, grocery shopping, cooking, and household costs.

It is important that you exercise caution and do the research if you are considering house sharing. Be certain to ask potential housemate applicants for references. Perhaps you have friends that might desire to share a home with you. You may even be interested in turning your current home into a shared residence. That would certainly reduce the stress level associated with the changes.

The National Shared Housing Resource Center (*nationalsharedhousing.org*) offers listings of various programs. Match-up programs help home providers find a compatible home seeker to pay rent or possibly provide services in exchange for a reduction in rent. Shared living residences involve a number of unrelated people living cooperatively. The directory link allows you to explore programs on a state-by-state basis.

Frugality & Your Home Utilities

There are a variety of ways to be frugal with your utilities at home. Rick Economides, author of *America's Cheapest Family,* suggests the following:

- Use an evaporative cooler instead of an air conditioner. Doing so can cost you 66% less. Also, a large ceiling fan may work well.
- Consider a programmable thermostat.
- An energy efficient wood stove can reduce your heating costs.
- Wear extra layers in the winter.
- Purchase a water heater jacket.
- Install additional insulation, especially in your attic.

Frugal Resources to Help You Stay in Your Home

There are a number of resources and organizations out there to assist you in remaining in your community and staying in your home.

As an example, East Rock Village in New Haven, CT, is a nonprofit committed to provide its members with services and confidence they need to remain active members of their community. For a nominal membership fee you can receive home maintenance services, transportation, exercise venues, and companionship. You do not need to be disabled.

Other resources include Volunteer Match (*volunteermatch.org*), Volunteers of America (*voa.org*), and Faith in Action (*fianationalnetwork.org*).

AARP offers frugal suggestions for modifying your home to make it more comfortable.

Be certain to log onto the Senior Corps (*seniorcorps.gov*) website to see the variety of services available in their Senior Companion Program.

How About a Vacation Home

Five years ago, my wife and I fell in love with the Southwest. We had already been retired for 7 years. At that time the economy was just beginning the downturn. Real estate prices were still relatively high.

We began to think about the possibility of buying property in Arizona. We have close friends that had already done so. In fact, they decided to relocate in Scottsdale, Arizona permanently. Ultimately we bought a condominium there. At the time of this writing, our condo is worth about 40% less than we paid. Fortunately, we were able to readily afford the price we paid at the time and I paid cash for the property.

At the time of this writing, Money Magazine suggested that the prices of condos in long-time favorite retiree areas have come down dramatically. Those areas include Napa, California, Tucson, AZ, Naples and Miami, Florida, and Hilton Head, South Carolina.

Given the current state of property values, you would think that purchasing a vacation home is a no-brainer. That is not necessarily the case. There are a variety of issues that you need to consider.

Given that this is a book about frugality, the main question is: Can I truly afford to do this? If you are considering paying cash for your retirement vacation home, be sure you have enough savings left over to cover at least a year's worth of living expenses. A condo usually requires a monthly maintenance fee payable to the homeowners association.

In addition, you will need to think about how much use you will get out of the property. Yes, there is always the possibility of renting out your place, but income from renting can fluctuate. The rental site *homeaway.com* says that rental property has a tenant fewer than 20 weeks per year. And, you may have to pay a fee to a property manager. If you are considering a condo, you will also need to ascertain whether the development allows renting.

Need Money? Check Out Reverse Mortgages

If you are in a precarious situation with your finances and you may have to sell your beloved home, consider a reverse mortgage. This is another frugal way to realize your retirement dreams.

Basically, this is a special loan situation designed for people over the age of 62 who own their homes outright or have a low balance remaining on their current mortgage.

A reverse mortgage allows the homeowner to take the equity out of their home and use it for other purposes. You do not need any income to qualify, and you can remain in your home as long as you live. The lending institution actually sends you a check each month, or you can choose to utilize the reverse mortgage as a line of credit. There is actually no loan-taking place since no monthly repayments are required.

The mortgage comes due when the last living borrower dies or the property is sold. That means that your heirs would be dealing with the disposition of your property. The most important consideration here is that you cannot outlive this loan. Also, your estate is not liable if the value of the property declines. The bank assumes that risk.

Transportation

When we acquired our second home in Arizona, our goals included not having to perform home maintenance tasks, and being able to walk or bike as much as possible, especially when it came to doing daily local errands such as small grocery purchases, going to the hair stylist, taking Yoga classes, going to the post office and library. We wanted to leave the car behind when feasible. We purchased an over-55 condo located on the edge of town. We can shop, go to the library, and do most other tasks easily. Ultimately, that reduces our gas expense by a fair amount.

As you know, a car is expensive. The cost of ownership, which includes auto insurance, maintenance and repairs, and depreciation all adds up. And, do not forget the cost of buying the car. Many retirees are buying property where public transportation is available. We bought a $5,000 economical car for Arizona that was in like-new condition, and we cancel the auto insurance when we're away in an effort to be frugal. This proved to be a cost-effective move over the long-term as opposed to renting a car.

Buying a smaller vehicle can be a smart move when the time comes. This is especially the case when the cost of repair rises sharply.

Here are some ideas for keeping the cost of owning a vehicle down:

- Fuel-efficient cars and hybrids do indeed keep fuel costs down.
- If you need a truck, either borrow or rent.
- Try to pay cash in an effort to keep the total cost down.
- Keep your car well maintained. That may very well keep the costs of repairs down.
- Find a good mechanic.

The following suggestions from the Insurance Information Institute relate to saving money on automobile insurance.

- Make certain that you comparison-shop. The same coverage can vary by hundreds of dollars. However, only do business with a highly-rated company.
- Consider dropping collision and/or comprehensive coverage on older cars.

- Cars that are expensive to repair have higher insurance costs.
- Take advantage of low-mileage discounts. Some companies offer discounts if you drive fewer than a set number of miles a year.
- Find out about safe-driver discounts.
- Maintain good credit. In some states your credit score may influence your insurance rate.
- Take a higher deductible. This action could significantly reduce your collision and comprehensive costs.

When the time comes to replace a vehicle, be careful. One of my hobbies is cars. I've learned over the years to be rather mistrustful of car dealers. At this point, I am very cautious about such transactions as trading in a car. It is always a frugal approach to get as much as you can for your old car. So, be sure to visit *nadaguides.com* or *edmunds.com* to get a realistic idea about the trade-in value of the vehicle. It is important to include all the details of the vehicle such as mileage and options and general overall condition. The website will also inform you of what to expect if you sell the car privately. You will then have somewhat of an informed approach when you are ready.

When you approach a dealer to trade in your car, you will be empowered if you have the preceding information. I've found that under no circumstances should you accept the dealer's first offer. They may attempt to assess you unnecessary reconditioning charges, mileage charges, and other fine print charges. My own experience has been such that I've always gotten a better price when I've sold the vehicle privately. *Craigslist.org* works very well for re-sales. You may even consider placing classified ads in local newspapers and other locally published ad sources. Some of those may even be free.

When the time comes to buy a new vehicle, visit *carwoo.com* or *truecar.com*. Both of those sites will allow you to obtain a price quote online without revealing any contact info before negotiations. If you do visit a dealership, you will be armed with prices from various dealers. That may give you a better footing.

Speaking of timing, the best time to purchase a car is usually at the end of the month. At that time, dealers are scrambling to meet sales quotas. Salespeople often gain bonuses during those times.

Finally, when you do make a purchase, be frugal about it even more. That is, the dealer may attempt to sell you a variety of aftermarket items that many experts say makes no sense to purchase. Those items include fabric protectors, aftermarket security systems, and extended warranties and other add-ons. For example, a built-in GPS can cost a great deal more money than a good portable unit.

Finally, Some frugal suggestions for operating your vehicle are as follows:

Be certain to rotate your tires as recommended. In the long run, this will save you money in terms of tire replacement.

When you fill your gas tank, tighten the gas cap until you hear a click. Loose-fitting caps can reduce gas mileage.

If you pay for gas by credit card, do your research. Certain cards offer higher rewards for gas purchases.

Try to maintain steady speeds when you drive. Sudden starts and stops can reduce mileage by as much as 5%. In addition, try to limit the amount of time that your car idles.

Log onto *gasbuddy.com* or *gasprice.com*. I use these websites to keep tabs on where to find the best deals on gas prices.

If you need car repairs, be sure to obtain several estimates. You will be surprised by the variations in costs. These differences become even more apparent if you approach an independent mechanic. The only exception I've found is in the case of oil changes. Dealers may offer special prices in an effort to sell you some other services.

CHAPTER 11: FRUGAL RELOCATION

As previously mentioned, it is crucial that you examine your personal finances and goals. If you've decided to relocate to pursue your passions, try to determine if a particular location will serve your lifestyle preferences. If you are relocating with a spouse, be certain that the new location serves all of your interests. That is, although the environment may be very idyllic, are there activities that will satisfy your intellectual and cultural interests. Be realistic about the long-term impact of a potential move. Check out transportation facilities and cultural and entertainment venues.

When my wife and I purchased a second residence in Arizona, the above considerations were very important. Our condominium is an over-55 community with no pets allowed. We wanted a peaceful location with beautiful grounds. We can walk 7 minutes to the center of our town to dine and be entertained. Further, we live across the street from a medical complex if we need those services. We do not have to drive for many daily chores (supermarket, salons, hardware store), which in turn makes this location a frugal alternative for us in terms of saving gas. Accessibility to commercial establishments may be a major consideration for you.

John Howells, in his book entitled *Where to Retire*, suggests the following requirements he considers essential for successful retirement relocation.

- safety – Are you able to walk through your neighborhood without looking over your shoulder?
- climate – Will temperatures and weather patterns match your lifestyle?

- social compatibility – Will you fit in with your neighbors and find common interests (if that is important to you)? You may also want to consider if your neighbors have similar cultural and social backgrounds.
- distance from family and friends – Are you going to be in a far away location where nobody wants to visit you?
- volunteer opportunities – If you would like to volunteer are there enough options to keep you busy?
- transportation – Does your new location offer inter-city bus transportation or train connections? Many small towns have none making you dependent on an automobile.
- a lively downtown – Does your town have a town center with restaurants, shopping, and places to meet friends?
- your favorite vacation destination – If you decide to relocate to your vacation spot, you need to ask yourself whether you will be happy living there year-round? Is there enough to do or will you be bored?
- Are senior services, in addition to free meals, available? Those services would include volunteer opportunities and education.

If you intend to work during retirement, will that affect the location of your new residence? That is, will your income be tied to a particular location?

It may worth your while to take a vacation to an area that you are interested in, especially if it is a distant location. You do not want to make a costly relocation mistake. A helpful way to learn about an area is to have conversations with local residents inquiring about opportunities to pursue your interests.

By the way, if you would like to relocate and continue to work, see the chapter in this book titled, "You Can Still Work" for suggestions.

Frugal Retirement Communities

Once you've gone through the criteria for where you would like to live, you may want to explore life in a retirement community. There are frugal communities out there.

Speaking from my own experience, owning a condominium in an over-55 community in Arizona has created a great retirement lifestyle. We live among retirees that are similarly active, enjoy amenities such as a fully maintained pool, and have many of our monthly utility costs included in the low $200 homeowners association fee including cable TV and water.

It is well worth comparing the ongoing costs of residing in a retirement community compared with the costs of remaining in your own home. Compile a yearly summary of home costs, which would include utilities and insurance as well as an estimate of maintenance. Be certain to analyze exactly what items are included in your HOA charges.

If you find a complex that you are interested in, be certain to fully investigate any and all homeowner fees and past records for special assessments. Those assessments usually occur when a capital improvement becomes necessary, such as roof replacement or foundation repairs. Examine operating budgets for the community. Obviously, the more services and facilities offered by the community, the higher the charge is likely to be. Normally, residents do have input into budgetary matters. The larger the complex, the more the costs are divided among residents so that ultimately, individual costs are lower. The residents of our complex are very frugal and often discourage improvements that are conceived as frivolous. It is important to note that the community homeowners association is normally responsible for all external repairs. So, for example, we had a roof leak in our condo in Arizona that literally cost thousands of dollars to repair. Our share of the cost was zero. The homeowner is responsible only for interior repairs and maintenance. In and of itself, the savings on exterior repairs can definitely be substantial with HOA (homeowners association) management.

In our community, you can purchase a unit at the time of this writing for under $100,000. There are 55 units with 1,000 square feet of living space including two master bedrooms and two master bathrooms. Children and grandchildren are readily welcomed as guests. Since no pets are allowed, it is a quiet environment. Residents in our complex are there because they prefer this type of setting. We have a beautiful pool. Some communities offer a gym. Sun City West has more than 15,000 homes on 7,100 acres with a population of around 40,000. Many communities, especially larger ones, have on-site management and even serve meals and offer medical care. You may also find security services.

There are many retirees that would prefer to live in mixed generation neighborhoods where one is surrounded by young children and teenagers. They find younger children fun to be with.

Many retirement communities offer a wide variety of activities, if that is what you want. Golf may be available. Several Arizona communities keep the cost of a round of golf to a reasonable $30 including a cart.

You may also find at your disposal recreation centers, and craft centers and clubhouses. Check out Del Webb (*delwebb.com*) as they have locations around the country.

Keeping in mind the emphasis on frugality, there are certain suggestions to consider in a retirement community. Richard

Andrews, in his book, *Don't Buy Your Retirement Home Without Me*, suggests the following ideas to think about:
1. Are the common areas clean and well maintained? In our complex in Arizona those areas are beautiful.
2. Are the facilities in good repair?
3. Do things such as lifts, pools, and spas work?
4. Are the residents of the community happy?
5. Is the landscaping well kept?

Pocket Neighborhoods
By a show of hands, how many of you have heard about pocket neighborhoods?

According to AARP, you will be hearing more about these increasingly popular housing options. They generally consist of a dozen or so compact houses or apartments that share common or green space. That might include a walkway, garden, or a courtyard. The setup is such that neighbors have opportunities to interact and form relationships. Pocket homes usually have an open floor plan and are newly constructed, oftentimes with separate parking garages so that neighbors do not pull into garages and disappear. Homes may be close together and can range in size from 1,000–2,000 feet. Because of the smaller size, maintenance tasks are less and cost less.

Pocket neighborhoods can be a great path to follow if you are considering downsizing, and if you find a location in town, you can walk to movies and restaurants. Indeed, another frugal alternative.

Another Alternative: Mobile Home Living
For many people, a mobile home presents an ideal way to live with all the comforts and conveniences that you would require, with a minimum investment and without the high real

estate taxes. Most mobile home communities require a monthly fee, which includes water, trash disposal, and sewer.

Depending on the location, not all mobile home parks are inexpensive. Some charge as much for rental space as an apartment. Be certain to check listings online at such sites as *mhbay.com* or *usdirectory.com*. Most parks cater to couples or singles who desire exceptional personal safety, friendly neighbors, and a club-like atmosphere. The better parks will have pools, recreation and social halls, and barbecue areas. The more luxurious parks can offer tennis courts, clubhouses, and hot tubs.

The cost of owning a mobile home can also vary greatly. Used models can cost $20,000 while new units can start at $65,000. Sizes vary by length and width. It is important that you know your financial limitations and buy what you can afford. Be aware of potential depreciation and the high cost of financing.

You may also want to consider buying a mobile home and the land it sits on. Certain developments may be selling lots rather than renting them, as well as the mobile home on that lot. It is important that you actually hold the title to the land rather than buying into a revocable lease. A mobile home on your own land can be a very frugal housing alternative. Actually, the total investment can be minimal as long as you can effectively deal with the setup work.

Make sure that you carefully check all local regulations along with the availability of electricity, water, and sewer hookups.

RV (Recreational Vehicle) Communities

In the chapter in this book on frugal travel ideas, I discuss in detail the idea RV travel. You could take this idea on step further and consider living in your RV in an RV community.

During our 40 years of RVing, we visited many such parks and became very familiar with the associated lifestyle.

Living in such a community does not mean you have to give up your desire for wanderlust. On the contrary, many RVers stay in the same communities throughout the year. Basically, you would become a "full time" RVer.

This lifestyle allows you to take your home with you without the stress of airline or train travel, and you even have your own bathroom and kitchen.

In addition, you are afforded the opportunity to meet a lot of people and have a variety of adventures along the way. Most of these communities are well established and have regular meetings and will instill a sense of neighborhood. I suggest that you consider a variety of factors before you select an RV community including location, your interests, and your general plan for retirement.

Relocation Overseas

If you've traveled internationally, you may be interested in relocating to another country. For many people, retiring overseas is an exciting dream. Many countries do indeed offer better social programs and healthcare services than the United States. And you may be able to find a country where the cost of living is substantially less. It is easy to understand why many U.S. citizens make the move.

Does the thought of overseas relocation excite you? Are you invigorated to the point that you might even consider the following the Jeffrey Webber tenets: reinvention, self-rediscovery, and self re-definition?

There are many factors to consider within the context of your personal circumstances. Many of you will prioritize your needs differently. You must determine for yourself what is most important and where you have some flexibility.

Perhaps you may want to consider part-time overseas retirement. It may be overwhelming to consider selling all of your personal possessions, leaving your family and friends and beginning a new life. If you are like us, we would never want to sell our primary residence because we love it. As well, you may be intimidated by the distance between you and your grandchildren. In addition to the previous reasons, you may indeed have some budgetary restraints, especially if your nest egg has taken a beating in recent years. You may be able to rent a seasonal place abroad or even rent your place back home. By the way, another advantage to part-time overseas retirement is that you do not have to worry about foreign residency options of visas. You only have to do this if you expect to reside permanently in that country.

Kathleen Peddicord, author of *How to Retire Overseas* (Hudson Street Press, 2009), has come up with a reference list for you to consider regarding a potential move. I highly recommend reading this book if you are considering international relocation. Here is part the list:
- cost of living – Are your income sources enough to support this lifestyle?
- cost of housing – Buying or renting is a consideration.
- Climate – What kind of climate do you prefer?
- healthcare – Your age and any preexisting conditions are two important factors when it comes to qualifying for international health insurance.
- infrastructure
- accessibility to the US – Will you be able to travel back to the U.S. if necessary?
- language – You may need to learn a second language, or at least some important phrases.

- culture, recreation and entertainment – Can you do the things you enjoy in your new location?
- taxes – Where will you derive your income while retired overseas?
- safety

In her book, Peddicord recommends several international retirement locations where you can live cheaply.

1. Cuenca, Ecuador – The author feels that this is the most affordable place you would want to live in Latin America. Here you can enjoy city life with all the amenities and conveniences that make it comfortable. She feels that Cuenca affords you the best quality of life buy for the money.

2. Chiang Mai, Thailand – In the world's second most affordable retirement haven, a couple can live for as little as $1,055 per month if you rent, and even less if you own. Bicycle transportation is very easy here.

3. Leon, Nicaragua – Leon is one of the oldest cities in the Americas (founded in 1524), and life here remains simple, unhurried, and relaxed. As Leon has most of what would need centrally located, the author suggests that you may not need to invest in a car. She states that you could probably live here on a budget of $1,200–$1,400 per month.

4. Las Tablas, Panama – This is the author's top recommendation for beachfront retirement where the cost of renting is low enough to accommodate anyone's budget. There is also first-class medical care and facilities. This city can also be a tax haven for those wishing to minimize their taxes.

5. Languedoc-Roussillon, France – Beyond Paris, the southwest part of this country can be highly affordable. The area is colorful, eclectic, and very amenable to

retirees. There are many expats of several nationalities living there. You will find a typically French village atmosphere. The cost of renting in this area can be modest with a monthly rental of 400 to 600 euro quite realistic.

6. Medelin, Columbia – This area is becoming an emerging retirement haven. Costs of living and renting are low. You can rent a two-bedroom apartment in a new building for $700 or $800 per month.

The author also suggests other locations that would come under the heading of "Luxury Living On a Budget." Those destinations include Paris, Buenos Aires, and Kuala Lampur.

In an effort to present you with as many choices as possible if you are considering international relocation, The Street (*thestreet.com*) a digital financial media company, suggests the following countries for their inexpensive living:

- Panama – Real estate prices and rentals are very reasonable.
- Mexico – At the time of this writing, coastal homes can be purchased for less than $170,000 and the destination is drivable.
- Columbia – The healthcare system is one of the highest rated.
- New Zealand - A reputation for healthy living.
- Nicaragua – Doctor visits can cost as much as 60% less than the U.S.
- Spain – great cultural opportunities and a well-developed modern infrastructure.
- Thailand – A reasonable cost of living along with vibrant cultural and entertainment options and lots of

English-speaking people make this country a good choice.

In her book, *Nextville,* Barbara Corcoran has some suggestions regarding whether your nest egg will go further overseas. You should closely examine the following:

1. Cost of Living – In Southeast Asia and Central America the cost of living can be half of what it is in the U.S. On a budget that might force you to scrounge here, you could live by the water and eat at the best restaurants and have maid service.
2. Exchange Rate – Be certain to check out the exchange rates to see how stable they have been.
3. Taxes – Sometimes you can save a bundle on property taxes because many countries encourage foreigners to buy land with the potential elimination of those property taxes. Check whether the United States has a tax treaty with the country you are moving to as that determines whether the income you earn in that country is exempt from U.S. taxes.
4. Healthcare – Although you will not be able to rely on Medicare overseas, medical care can be much less expensive. Often you can join a state-sponsored medical plan for a few hundred dollars a year.
5. Local Retirement Benefits – Many countries offer discounts and special benefits to pensioners who move there. Check the specific country's website or their tourism office.

You may want to also consider accessibility. That is, how easy will it be for you to from your new home to your family, in case of an emergency or an occasional visit? Hopefully, there is an airport nearby.

In addition, it is important to think about your communication skills in your new country. Will you speak the language well enough to obtain the services you need? Is there telephone service and Internet access? Are there people who speak English nearby?

Then there is the safety concern. Check whether your new country is stable and welcomes foreigners.

Locating Affordable States to Retire

A most important consideration for you in terms of a frugal relocation in this country would be to find a tax-friendly state, if there is such a place.

The major taxes that you would be faced with during retirement would be income, property, and sales taxes. Some states do not tax social security. Other states may exempt income from certain pensions. You may also find that some states only tax out of state pensions.

States without income taxes include Florida, Texas, Washington, Alaska, Wyoming, and South Dakota.

Property taxes are very high in the Northeast. I can attest to that since we own a residence property in Connecticut. Certain southern state residents pay much less. I can attest to that since we own a residence in Arizona.

By the way, Montana, Alaska, New Hampshire, Oregon, and Delaware have no sales tax.

The three most popular states for retirement at the time of this writing are Florida, California, and Arizona (my personal favorite), in that order. Obviously, those states share one thing in common: enjoyable winter temperatures.

If you are looking to relocate domestically, falling home prices can create a bargain for you. Retirees may now be able to afford homes in places they were priced out of only a year ago.

Not every place will feel affordable depending on how wealthy you are.

U.S. News has come up with a list of 10 bargain retirement spots. These are locations where average home sale prices were falling fast, at the time of this writing.

1. Portland, OR
2. Tallahassee, FL
3. Tucson, AZ
4. Wake Forest, NC
5. Cathedral City, CA
6. Wahiawa, HI
7. Weatherford, TX
8. Dover, DE
9. Sycamore, IL
10. St. Charles, MD

At the time of this writing, *Money Magazine* suggested a list of the best places to retire. Needless to say, much of the basis for their decisions was predicated on frugality. Here are some examples:

- Marquette, MI - Along with average home prices at $145,000 and the state income tax at 4.3%, Marquette has a lively downtown and proximity to Lake Superior.
- Cape Coral, FL – Average home prices here are only $95,000 along with no state income tax. It is a paradise for water lovers with 400 miles of canals.
- Boise, ID – Average home prices here are $120,000. Boise has a very active cultural scene with theaters and museums and the city is surrounded by mountains and a river.
- Danville, KY – Many districts in Danville are on the National Register of Historic Places and there are plenty

of activities to keep busy. Average property tax at this time is only $880.

- Weatherford, TX – Located 33 miles from Fort Worth, Weatherford has maintained it's own identity, which is wrapped up with horses. Numerous horse events take place here. In addition, the downtown are is charming and boating takes place on Lake Weatherford. Average home prices are $150,000.

I do not mean to inundate you with lists. However, *The Street* (the online financial journal) has come up with a list of a list of the cheapest (lowest cost of living) cities in the country. The 10 cities below offer the lowest cost-of-living levels of some 300 communities surveyed. Each cost of living score is less than 90% of the overall U.S. average. They include:

1. Harlingen, TX
2. Memphis, TN
3. McAllen, TX
4. Fayetteville, AR
5. Ardmore, OK
6. Tempe, TX
7. Ashland, OH
8. Conway, AR
9. Pueblo, CO
10. Pryor Creek, OK

According to AARP, *TopRetirements.com* came up with a list of the 10 worst states for retirement in terms of fiscal health and climate. Here's the list:

1. Illinois – poor fiscal health
2. California – financial disarray
3. New York – very high taxes
4. Rhode Island – worst state in the northeast financially
5. New Jersey – high taxes and pension funding issues

6. Ohio – high unemployment
7. Wisconsin – high property taxes
8. Massachusetts – high cost of living and property taxes
9. Connecticut – high property taxes and Social Security tax
10. Nevada – foreclosure capital of the world

A recent article from *kiplinger.com*, suggests that there are ten states that they consider to be "tax hells." These states offer higher than average taxes across the board or do not exempt much retirement income from taxation. If you are on a fixed income high income taxes can definitely eat into a nest egg.

The list of states includes:

- Vermont – There are very few exemptions for retirement income in this state. The property tax is among the ten highest in the nation.
- Minnesota – Social Security income is taxed to the same extent it is taxed on your federal return.
- Nebraska – No tax breaks are offered for Social Security benefits. Real estate is assessed at 100% of fair market value.
- Oregon – This state imposes the highest tax rate in the nation on taxable income over $250,000.
- California – Residents of this state pay some of the highest income taxes in the U.S. State and local taxes can be as high as 9.25%.
- Maine – A variety of income taxes are required.
- Iowa – Portions of retirement plan distributions can be taxed as high as 8.98%.
- Wisconsin – This state taxes most (except Social Security) pension and annuity income the same way the federal government does.

- New Jersey – It is said that New Jersey combined state and local tax burden is the highest in the nation.
- Connecticut – Social Security income is only excluded from taxes if gross income is $50,000 or less.

By the way, I highly recommend that you read John Howells latest book, *Where to Retire*. He discusses in detail America's best and most affordable palaces to relocate with special attention to climate and geography. States discussed include Florida, California, Arizona, Southeast Coast states, Gulf Coast states, and the Pacific Northwest states.

Organizations

FIND UTOPIA (*findutopia.com*) – This site consolidates resources to assist you in researching locations to live and retire. Information is included on cost of living, housing prices, and retirement communities. The suggested sequence of steps is made up of links relating to defining your goals, finding the best places to live, and information on various cities.

IDEAL PLACES TO RETIRE (*ideal-places-to-retire.com*) – This site offers detailed information on a variety of locations around the world. The author encourages you to fulfill life long dreams that may have been on hold. Hopefully you will be empowered by the information provided.

CHAPTER 12: STAYING HEALTHY & SAVING MONEY

When you put things in perspective, don't you think the most realistic goal for those of us in our "Third Age" is to be happy and healthy? Of course, there are many factors that influence the achievement of that broad goal. Certainly, being happy can contribute greatly to being healthy. If you have kids, worrying about their welfare may detract from the happiness component in terms of the stress factor.

In my first book, *The New Professional Person's Retirement Lifestyle,* I discuss in detail the importance of developing a plan for retirement that you will definitely follow. As I indicated in the introduction of this book, knowing your projected income in relation to the goals you've devised, along with your expenses can make for a happy retirement. And I do believe that this happiness may keep you healthier.

Let's look at some ways you can save some money in terms of staying healthy from a physical standpoint.

Medical Suggestions

As we all know, the cost of healthcare and associated insurance is creating havoc on our budgets. At the time of this writing, the Supreme Court has decided that the Affordable Care Act can stand. Time will tell what costs will be for individuals to purchase health insurance.

Hopefully you have medical insurance with reasonable coverage or are eligible for Medicare. During all the years I worked as a public school teacher, I never contributed to Social Security since I was not required to do so. Recently I turned 65.

Since I am not eligible for Medicare (not having contributed to S.S.), I was allowed to continue with my current healthcare plan. The point is, you must have some kind of coverage.

Be as certain as you can, that your health insurance claims are handled appropriately. Do not count on the insurance company and the medical provider completing the process correctly. Any mistakes in the process could result in rejected coverage. This is especially the case where there is lack of communication.

If you are interested in a free eye exam and a year of follow-up by volunteer ophthalmologists, and you are over 65, log onto *EyeCareAmerica.org*.

The Lions Club International, the Sertoma Hearing Aid Recycling Program, and the Starkey Hearing Foundation's Hear Now Program all sponsor recycling campaigns that help the financially needy obtain hearing aids.

Try to understand your coverage, especially when it comes to physicals, deductibles, and types of physicians. Incidentally, feel free to ask your doctor for a discount before your appointment. You may also want to think about arranging special extended payment terms Try to negotiate directly with the doctor, not the office personnel, before the treatment. Speak candidly with your doctor (or service provider) regarding your individual circumstances, particularly if you are living on a limited fixed income or do not have reasonable coverage. If your initial request for a discount is rejected, inquire about paying cash for your services. Point out that your cash payment may save them credit card fees. On that basis, you be eligible for a discount. I think it is important to remember that insurance companies negotiate with healthcare providers on a regular basis. You may be successful at this as well. In addition, an assistance program may be available. You may even be eligible for free treatment and medication if you qualify for a medical study at *clinicaltrials.gov* or from a local medical school. Be certain to check the study's credentials.

The Healthcare Blue Book (*healthcarebluebook.com*) is a free consumer guide that will help you determine fair prices in your local area for healthcare services including surgery, hospital stays, doctor visits, tests, and much more. This is especially significant if you have a high deductible or you are not fully covered by insurance. At the website, all you need to do is type in keywords and search available services and prices. They suggest that you call your insurance provider and compare their price for the service before you begin your search.

Finally, make sure that you keep all of your records in case there any questions about the nature of the claim.

Frugal Dental Suggestions

Some common sense ways to save money on dental care are as follows:

- Schedule regular cleanings. Have your teeth cleaned every six months by a professional. This will catch any existing problems and help to avoid future problems.
- Purchase a discount dental plan. This can be a good path to follow if you do not have coverage.
- Ask for a cash discount. Check with your dentist for a discount by paying with cash.
- Set up a payment plan. This approach will spread out the cost dental work.
- Go to a dental school. Supervised dental students will perform the work. This could save you a substantial amount of money.
- Stay on top of the day-to-day care of your teeth. Brush and floss regularly. Replace your toothbrush when necessary. Cut down on sugary foods and drinks.

Prescriptions

As you know, the out-of-pocket costs of prescription drugs are extreme if you do not have coverage. There are some cost saving alternatives to the local drugstore.

If you search "discount prescriptions" on Google, you will find a number of discount online merchants such as *drugstore.com* or *prescriptiongiant.com* or *pharmnet.com*. Purchasing prescriptions this way depends on how comfortable you are with that process.

If you are a member of Costco or Sam's Club, you may realize substantial savings over your local drugstore. Judy from Scottsdale, AZ reports a savings of $5 per month on her regular prescription. *Costco.com* refills prescriptions 24 hours a day and can be delivered anywhere in the United States. In fact, you can request that your doctor write prescriptions from the discount prescription lists from big-box or warehouse stores.

In addition, if you have prescription coverage as part of your health insurance, your doctor may able to write a prescription for a 3-month supply. The end result is a savings on the co-pay amount. Another hint is to try to obtain a double dosage of the drug so you can split the pill in half.

Don't forget the generic drug alternative. At the time of this writing, you could get a 30-day supply of some generic drugs for $4 without any program enrollment fees at Walmart, Sam's Club, and Target. Find local offerings at *medtipster.com*. Before you leave your doctor's office, ask if the medication prescribed has a generic. If it doesn't, follow up by asking if there's a drug with a generic that would work as well for your condition. It's a simple question that could save a lot. At the time of this writing, a generic alternative to Lipitor, the most popular-selling drug, became available. The cost of this generic is about one-half of Lipitor. I am saving a great deal of money on my prescription plan coverage for this drug at this point in time.

There is some evidence to indicate that properly stored medication can be effective long after the expiration date. Check with your doctor.

By the way, most doctors' offices are well stocked with free samples of prescription and over the counter medications. Don't forget to ask. You may be pleasantly surprised and could receive a month's supply. Further, check with your doctor and local pharmacy to see if any rebates or coupons are available for the prescriptions that you use. You may not be aware of the fact that pharmacies do receive samples. Check to see if any of the over-the counter medications that you need are available.

If you've used up your allotted coverage for prescriptions or you do not have drug coverage, be certain to shop around to obtain prices. Base prices can vary from pharmacy to pharmacy. Another suggestion, which I frequently do, is to split pills. Check with your doctor to see if this is an option for your. Pill splitters are very inexpensive.

Finally, if you do not have prescription coverage, check to see if you are eligible for a prescription discount card that emanates from an organization that you belong to such as AARP or AAA. You might even consider shop around for a paid pharmacy discount card. The cost of the membership could readily be recovered from your savings. Some drug manufacturers do have hardship programs, which would allow you to get your medication for free or a reduced cost.

Long-Term Healthcare Insurance

Long-term care insurance can save you a great deal of money in the event that you need care in a nursing home, assisted living facility, or in your own home. LTC will also make it much less stressful for your adult children. They would have less to worry about in terms of taking care of you and their own families. Current nursing home and assisted living costs can range from $50,000 to $100,000 a year and more depending on the nature of the accommodations.

Many people believe that Medicare will pay for this care. That is not necessarily the case. Medicare requires that your net worth be very low before the government will pick up the tab for a nursing home. Full Medicare coverage in a nursing home may only last 20 days. Beyond that term, you may have to contribute to the cost of your care. The reality is that Medicare will only provide limited assistance for your long-term health needs.

Here are some suggestions for saving money on long-term healthcare insurance.

- Attempt to find a group policy for long term care, as this is usually less expensive.
- Buy as early as possible since the premiums increase as you age. My wife and I purchased our policies when we turned 50. At the time of this writing I am 66. Most experts agree that the best time to purchase long-term healthcare is before the age of 59. Before you reach the age of 61, it is most likely that you will pay $2,500 a year or less. In addition, you do not want to risk being turned down due to a pre-existing condition.
- Buy a policy with a waiting period for benefits.
- Long-term care policies are available which only pay a percentage of costs.
- Always compare quotes. A company with the lowest premiums may actually have a record of frequent premium increases.
- Be certain that you buy insurance from a company with a stable financial history. You do want the company to be in business when you need them. Try to deal with a company that has an A.M. Best rating of A++ or A+.

Exercise

As part of an ongoing effort to think frugally, I have a great suggestion to help in the avoidance of medical bills. We have around 600 muscles in our body and it has proven beneficial to exercise those muscles. Of course, exercise does indeed work best in conjunction with proper rest and nutrition.

I firmly believe, as I have for most of my 66 years, in the benefits of exercise. I am thin, very healthy, and in general feel great. I rarely ever visit a physician's office other than for the purpose of regular maintenance. Each morning, when the weather is appropriate, I either ride my tandem bicycle with my wife, play tennis, hike, or speed walk around my neighborhood. When the weather is less than desirable, I will do 30 minutes on my treadmill. My wife and I took up ballroom dancing years ago and so we dance on a regular basis at dance studios who offer public events for as little as $5 per person. As well, dancing offers the additional benefit of making one happy.

As you probably realize, there are many exercise alternatives available to you. Some examples include:

- Walk at a mall. Take the stairs rather than the escalator or elevator.
- Utilize walking trails at local parks. My wife and I hike regularly at all local parks. Remember, walking is one of the most recommended exercises for seniors.
- Take inexpensive classes at your parks and recreation department or senior center.
- Visit your local YMCA.
- Join a gym with a senior discount. If you work out with a friend, you may feel more motivated.
- Buy an inexpensive exercise machine at a garage sale or on Craigslist.

- Do personal conditioning exercises in the comfort of your own home that emphasize stretching and muscle strengthening. See the AARP suggestions in the section below.
- Find an exercise program on TV. Check your local listings for workout programs. Additionally, you can check out exercise videos from you local library. Try to get a new video on a regular basis so you will not get bored with the same routine.
- Clean your house yourself. You would be surprised at the number of calories you can burn off through 30 minutes of housework.
- Turn on some music and practice your dancing. As previously indicated, my wife and I love ballroom dancing and we frequently practice our steps in the comfort of our own home. I can tell you, dancing is great exercise.
- As previously mentioned, if you own a bike, start riding. You can always purchase an inexpensive used bike at a garage sale.

AARP has come up with frugal ways to save money on your fitness activities. They include:

1. Aerobic Exercise – Suggestions include jumping rope, doing jumping jacks, jogging in place, hiking up and down, and bouncing on a mini-trampoline.
2. Strength Training – Put your back up against a wall, feet on the floor and knees bent at a 90-degree angle. Hold for 15 seconds and repeat. Push-ups are a good choice as well as curl-ups.
3. Build up your core strength – They recommend sit-ups, lying on your side and raising your torso off the floor,

and bird dogs (from all fours extend one arm out and raise the opposite leg behind you).
4. Bicycle Kicks – Lie on your back and pedal your legs in a cycling motion pointed at the ceiling.

By the way, if you are interested in joining a health club, see what the fees are on a pay-per-visit plan. Despite good intentions, many people only workout once per week and end up by overpaying with monthly or annual memberships.

If you would like to lose some weight and you own a smartphone, here is a cool suggestion: There are frugal apps available that will help you count calories. They are simple to use and encompass a variety of techniques. The apps include Lose it, MyFitness Pal, FatSecret, Meal Snap, and Fooducate. Some of these apps are actually free.

COMMUNITY SPORTS LEAGUES - Recently I observed a neighbor of mine playing softball in the Madison, CT Men's Over 60 Softball League. It was a fascinating experience. What I saw was a group of men ages 60–70 thoroughly enjoying a baseball game and supporting each other to the max. If one participant was having difficulty running, a designated runner would pitch in and vice versa. They were having a blast and saving money at the same time.

The team plays Tuesday and Thursday each week from April through October. The fee is only $40 dollars. Other classes offered by the town of Madison, CT for seniors includes:

- Men's Senior Golf League – offers play on different courses each week
- Seniors in Motion – designed to improve balance, strength and stability

- Fitness and Movement – low impact aerobics
- Exercise and Relaxation with Yoga – increasing circulation and relaxation
- Zumba – low-intensity exercise

Be certain to check the listings from your local parks and recreation department for similar reasonably priced offerings.

Eating Healthy and Saving Money

It is well known that eating healthy can keep your medical costs down. The trick is to keep the cost of healthy foods under control. Here are some tips:

1. Buy reduced price produce – As you know fresh produce can be expensive. Look for a reduced price rack at the grocery store. You can often purchase super ripe produce for a fraction of the regular price.

2. Buy frozen vegetables. They are usually a cheaper alternative.

3. Grow your own. I've been doing this for years. I know exactly how the veggies are raised. The costs are minimal, but the payoff can be large. Certainly, there is some work to be done, but there is a high level of satisfaction. It is important to select varieties that produce lots of food for the growing time, the effort required to raise the plants, and the growing space consumed. When you think about it, if there is a way to grow hundreds of pounds of food with just a few dozen seeds, that is a terrific return on your investment.

4. Pick your own. We reside near a large orchard that features a seasonal "pick your own" procedure. This produce is the freshest and usually the most economical. And, it is a fun thing to do, especially if you have grandchildren.

5. Shop for produce locally. Your local produce stand or farmer's market can be a great source for healthy bargains. You

can also find great deals through reduced price produce and end-of-the day specials.

I suggest that you visit the AARP food site (*aarp.org/food*). There you will find a variety of frugal recipes, tips on food preparation, and advice from food experts.

ADDITIONAL FRUGAL GROCERY TIPS

Many grocery shoppers who want to save money on groceries find that shopping once a week or less is the better way to go. Reasons for doing so include learning to become a smart shopper and spending less, as well as saving time and spending less on gas.

As you may already know, try not to do the bulk of your shopping in convenient stores as you may end up paying considerably more than you need to.

My wife spends a considerable amount of time examining newspaper supermarket ads in an effort to find sale prices on items that we need. If you can shop sale cycles, you will save money. Try to anticipate buying certain grocery items when they are on sale. When you do go grocery shopping, try to control impulse buying. Research has shown that a great deal of grocery shopping is based on impulse buying. By the way, don't forget dollar-store bargains when shopping for staples.

GROCERY SHOP ONLINE AND SAVE MONEY

Grocery shopping online is becoming more popular these days. There are lots of choices available to you. Some sites even offer free shipping. Aside from saving money on your groceries, the process can even be more appealing because you will be saving gas expenses. If you do not have a car, it can even be a better choice for you.

Online grocery sites include *amazon.com*, *walmart.com* and *alice.com*. In a recent survey at the time of this writing,

Consumers Reports Magazine found that Amazon was the most expensive of the above choices based on their grocery list. I have personally found this not to be the case. I suggest that you comparison-shop online in an effort to come up with the most frugal alternative. A recent grocery receipt would be very helpful here.

Alice offers free shipping for six items or more; Walmart's standard shipping is free for some items; Amazon does offer some promotion codes. *Walmart.com* does attempt to keep their prices the same as those in their stores.

OTHER MERCHANTS THAT WILL SAVE YOU MONEY

Money Magazine and I are big fans of Costco. I have been a member for at least twenty years and completely agree with the writers that if you intend to purchase meat or seafood, Costco's prices are simply unbeatable. You can readily save 15% to 30% over grocery store prices. Of course, in most cases you may have to buy a larger quantity, which is okay if you have the storage capabilities. It is important to note that Costco does not always necessarily have the lowest prices on groceries.

Shopping for items such as cereal, canned goods, and paper goods can save you money if you visit dollar stores. Then there are bargain food outlets such as Aldi's, Save-A-Lot, or Grocery Outlet. You may have to bag your own groceries, but you will save at least 50% off of regular grocery store prices.

By the way, if you are shopping for wine, be certain to check the store brand wines from Costco, Trader Joe's, and Whole Foods. They are often made with grapes from premier regions and are usually great deals.

Saving Money on Medicare Drug Plans

One of the strategies with Part D Medicare drug coverage is to compare plans. You may be paying more than you have to by a substantial amount. As it turns out, many enrollees do not compare available plans.

Most Part D drug plans change their costs and coverage's each calendar year. When the changes occur, the news can be either good or bad.

A main reason for comparing plans is that co-pays for the same drug can vary widely, even for the same drug. AARP has analyzed 2012 plans in three states and concluded that there are some big variations. They found huge disparities in co-pays for Liptor, Plavix, and Zyprexa.

They suggest that you use Medicare's online plan finder program at *medicare.gov*. When you enter your ZIP code, the names of the drugs you take, and how often you take them, the program will automatically find the plan in your area that covers the drugs you use at the least out-of-pocket expense. In addition, you can call the Medicare help line and request the assistance of a representative. Certainly you will want to consider service levels as well.

AARP suggests that you closely examine generic options. More generic drug alternatives are on the horizon. Those choices will offer other more frugal drugs replacing the three previously discussed.

Medicare estimates that about 2 million people who are eligible for subsidized coverage under Part D's Extra Help program are not enrolled. Eligibility requirements have eased. You can contact Social Security at *ssa.gov*.

CHAPTER 13: FRUGAL SITES AND ORGANIZATIONS FOR RETIREES

In my previous books I have attempted to emphasize the roles that various organizations have in making the retirement years more satisfying and enjoyable. It is important to note that they are able to do so frugally. These are membership organizations that faithfully serve those of us 50 years of age and over and attempt to improve our quality of life. Here are some examples:

AARP *(aarp.org)*
This organization has the largest membership of people over 50. They are attempting to lead a revolution the way people view and live life.

There a large variety of activities that you can sign up for at the website. At the time of this writing, the Personal Growth link was offering a free six-session art course on expressive drawing. The travel link presented information on which big cities were offering things to do at no charge, as well as where substantial discounts are available for those of you who are disabled.

A Discount link discusses discounts available for shopping, dining, health, fitness, and travel. Some of the more popular discounts offered include grocery coupons, various car rentals, restaurants, and even Walgreens.

Road Scholar (formerly Elderhostel) *(roadscholar.org)*
This nonprofit offers learning adventures for people over the age of 55. Worldwide programs include outdoor adventures to

study various cultures, history, the natural environment, and programs where you learn while helping others. They seek to empower adults to explore the world, interact with its people, and ultimately discover more about themselves. This is done through hands-on experience, which reflects emerging trends of our world.

A variety of great frugal programs are offered for under $600. Some of those have included

- A taste of the Cajun experience in food, music, and culture in Louisiana
- Hiking through North Georgia history
- Healthy self-indulgence in the California desert
- Biking in the Virginia Blue Ridge Mountains

Senior Corps (*seniorcorps.org*)

Here's a frugal way to keep on learning: join SeniorNet. This organization encourages seniors to utilize computer technology to enrich their lives. They offer hands-on computer courses in learning centers and online on a wide variety of topics.

Courses are led by instructors, are interactive, and last about six weeks. At the time of this writing, most online course fees are $109 and the average length per course is 24 hours. Areas of study include accounting, business, medical and healthcare, law, personal development, technology, and writing and publishing. Some of the more popular courses are Grant Writing, Creating Web Pages, Beginning Writers Workshop, and Becoming a Veterinary Assistant.

American Seniors Organization (*americanseniors.org*)

The goal of this organization is to provide seniors with choices and information they need to live healthier, wealthier lives. They offer their members choices to assist with Medicare, insurance, prescription discounts, auto and travel services, and fact-finding. They do indeed partner with a variety of companies to obtain discounts.

For a low fee of $15 per year, they will assist you with health plan services, finding reasonable auto insurance, life insurance, reverse mortgages, retirement homes, and assisted living, and a great deal more.

Seniors Coalition (*senior.org*)

This is a non-profit, non-partisan, education and issue advocacy organizations that represents the interests and concerns of America's senior citizens. The goal is protect the economic well-being of older Americans.

Seniors Home Exchange (*seniorshomeexchange.com*)

Here is a great way to frugally visit a place that you otherwise could not afford. Ultimately, you can save a great deal of money on vacation travel including hotels, meals, and car rentals.

Seniors Home Exchange is designed exclusively for the over-50 age group. Basically, you do a straight vacation exchange of your home. Many exchanges include car swapping.

At the time of this writing, there were 4,218 exchanges from 57 countries available. Those countries include Australia, South Africa, Spain, Turkey, and Portugal. In addition, there were offerings in practically every state.

The total cost of registering your home is $79 for 3 years or $100 for a lifetime listing.

All Things Frugal (*allthingsfrugal.com*)

This site features a large variety of frugal articles that will help you save money. At the time of this writing, tidbits were featured on inexpensive recipes, ways to cut cable TV expenses, making your own clothing to save money, and inexpensive window treatments along with home décor suggestions.

Frugal Retirement Living (*frugal-retirement-living.com*)

The authors of Frugal Retirement Living attempt encourage people " to retire and enjoy themselves."

They explain with a variety of frugal living links how they have succeeded in a creative and successful retirement over the past 17 years. Included in this discussion are their experiences living on a sailboat and an RV. There is also discussion on financial planning and the best places to retire.

USA.gov

This government-sponsored site lists a large number of links that provide resources for you to estimate your retirement benefits and learn about factors that could affect your retirement. You will find consumer information on pension plans, calculators, savings plans, Social Security information, working after retirement, and much more.

Money Over 55 (*moneyover55.about.com*)

This site offers practical information, which will allow you to take control of your spending habits. Budgeting techniques are presented in regards to developing better money skills. There are links to developing retirement expense worksheets, buying used cars, ways to save more money, and how to afford your passions during the retirement years.

Alliance for Retired Americans (*retiredamericans.org*)

A major goal of this organization, with a current membership of 3,000,000 people is to become a voice for older Americans in an effort to protect and preserve important programs relative to health and economic security of older

Americans. As you can imagine, Social Security and Medicare are a priority including healthcare reform. At their website, you can readily keep abreast of happenings on a state-by-state basis.

Seniorresource.com

This organization encourages seniors to successfully age in place and in general, cope with aging. Very useful subject matter includes understanding aging. They fully explain housing options.

Financial discussions include ways to reduce housing costs as well as how to secure additional income from home sharing. State-by-state resources are explored. Another link attempts to explain various laws.

American Automobile Association (*aaa.com*)

Just in case you are one of the few people who do not belong to AAA, please think carefully about joining.

Discounts galore are available with your membership cards. Those include dining, entertainment, healthcare, automotive purchase and repair, insurance, and all kinds of vacation deals.

frugalliving.about.com

This is a very useful site for frugal retirees that is regularly updated. The large number of links and advice offered will most definitely improve your financial picture.

The "getting started" link presents step-by-step suggestions for the process of creating a frugal budget, getting rid of debt, and ways to organize your finances.

In addition, you will find very timely advice for seniors in regards to healthcare, transportation, shopping, working, and money saving ways to save around the house. There is also advice offered on frugal ways to have fun.

serviceleader.org/virtual

If you have a desire to volunteer and would rather not travel, then, as previously described, virtual volunteering may be for you. Perhaps you are not physically able to travel or simply cannot afford to do so.

Be sure to check on *Serviceleader.org* for a variety of resources that will help you get started. Indeed, virtual volunteering is a frugal way to give back.

Generation America (*generationamerica.org*)
This membership organization offers access to exceptional discounts, benefits and services to people over the age of 50. Their philosophy is that members deserve the best products and services at significant savings. Some of this is accomplished by group buying power. Examples of discounts include roadside assistance plans, discount drug cards, hearing aids, car rentals, home and auto insurance, and certain legal services. In addition, financial advice is offered to members. The yearly membership dues is only $24.

Senior Job Bank (*seniorjobbank.org*)
This organization specializes in bringing together employers and qualified older job seekers. Their goal is to "provide a service that encompasses the full range of employment types and disciplines." At the site, you can easily seek out the job along with the location you are seeking.

The work can be part-time with flexible hours. There are also work-at-home positions available.

Babyboomers.org
This emphasis of this site is to find the best deals for boomers on things that boomers need. At the time of this writing, areas of discussion included:
- steps for finding the best elderly homecare

- technologies for the elderly
- dealing with medical bills
- long-term insurance
- medical bills and bankruptcy
- finding family caregivers

60 Plus Association (*60plus.org*)

This organization is an advocacy group devoted to free enterprise, less government, and less taxes approach to senior issues. They are often viewed as the conservative alternative to the AARP. Issues that the Association gets involved with include energy, healthcare, Social Security, and spending. Top priorities have been to end the federal estate tax and to save Social Security. One of their top spokesmen has been Pat Boone.

CHAPTER 14: PROFILES OF FRUGAL RETIREES

Sometimes, when you think of the "frugal retirement" terminology, you may be tempted to associate retirees who are living on the edge. That is, these are people who count every nickel and how they spend it. Perhaps they are living in unheated homes. In general, they may be spending very little not because they do not have the resources, but simply because they are cheap.

As I've indicated in previous chapters of this book, it is possible to adopt a frugal lifestyle and have fun as well.

The following examples profile various retirees who are indeed living frugally and doing what they want.

Gary Pierce

Gary Pierce retired in 1994 at the age of 49. From 1994 to 2002 he and his wife lived on a sailboat in the Caribbean. They cruised from Trinidad and Venezuela to the Virgin Islands spending around $1,000 a month while in the islands.

During the summers, they traveled the U.S. in an RV, which enabled them to find their permanent retirement home. They loved that lifestyle. They compared the cost of home ownership with park space rental of around $450 a month and you are seeing our beautiful country frugally.

When they retired to their boat, they went from 1,800 square feet to about 50 square feet. They live cheaply and well and feel that they are not controlled by their possessions.

Be sure to log onto Gary's retirement blog (*frugal-retirement-living.com/frugal-living-in-retirement-blog.html*).

Frugal tips abound. See more information about blogs later in this chapter.

Ray Freeman

Ray Freeman, author of the Frugal Retiree Newsletter (*thefrugalretiree.com*), feels that he lives very well on a fixed income. He has learned a great deal from other retirees at senior centers and coffee klatches. He suggests that you can think small. That is, a small house, small yard, small kitchen, small refrigerator, and small utility bills can lead to a fatter wallet and larger bank account. When you think big (cars and homes) you can easily end up with thin wallets and small savings accounts.

For entertainment, he and his wife review the local newspaper and attend local concerts and shows at local venues. Often times there are free concerts at local parks and informal tours at local historical sites.

They take advantage of the local dollar store and the numerous thrift stores in the area, particularly on the half-off days. They also utilize senior discounts.

For transportation, they drive around in a 12-year-old Subaru with 172,000 miles on the odometer. Gas and insurance costs are reasonable.

When dining out, they take advantage of discounts offered at local restaurants and *restaurant.com*. Ray feels strongly, as do I, that you should take advantage of Internet discounts.

Montez Mutzig

For as far back as I can remember, I've been interested in gardening as a hobby. It is, to say the least, a frugal hobby if you want it to be. It is also relaxing and quite rewarding.

After she was forced into retirement after a spinal injury, Montez Mutzig found herself at home with nothing to do. So, she turned to gardening. She attended classes and has hence turned cottage-style home into a work of art, the landscape dotted with color from a wide variety of plants and flowers. And it wasn't long before she was enrolling in classes to become certified as a Master Gardener. The front gardens, highlighted by flagstone steps and a walkway, are extensive. Lace bark elms, encased by flagstone beds create a focal point, and beds lining the front of the cottage have native flowers and perennials—from a new breed of daylilies (Kokomo Sunset) to purple Salvias and bright Indian Blankets, which are the state wildflower.

Mutzig has been able to use her love of gardening as an opportunity to once again help others. As a group, Tulsa County Master Gardeners partner with Tulsa Public Schools for workshops. Last fall alone, Mutzig said, they reached 13,000 kids. Mutzig also volunteers at a nature center, taking people on guided walks.

Akaisha and Billy Kaderli

These two people retired 20 years ago when they were only 38. They have traveled the world including such destinations as Guatemala, Vietnam, Australia, and New Zealand.

They live on less than $30,000 a year. Apparently, they have strong control over their cash flow. They feel that it is imperative to know how much you are spending not only in a year, but also in a day. They have eliminated all debt and cut expenses that don't provide meaningful and lasting value. For them, being in complete control of finances is an enhancement to self-confidence and is motivational. They live in areas of the world where the cost of living is low, but the beauty factors are high. When they need it, excellent medical care is available outside of the U.S. at reasonable prices.

Akaisha and Billy feel that the discipline attached to monitoring spending must be part of a new lifestyle approach. They don't live their lives in a vacation mode.

Barbara June

Some of the most interesting components of technology for people our age are blogs. In case you are not familiar with the term, a blog is a website that is hosted by an individual or a group of people who engage in an ongoing narrative about a single or a variety of subjects.

Living Richly in Retirement (*frugaltexasgal.com*) is a blog begun by a widow who considers herself a creative "frugalista." She is determined to have fun and live a full life on a fixed income through knitting, traveling, baking, and lots more.

Check out her suggestions and the associated blog posts that can offer very frugal suggestions. You will find a plethora of postings from people who have found interesting ways to make some money, to ways to save on healthcare costs, to suggestions about how to rekindle the spark in your retirement.

In addition, be sure to seek out other frugal retiree blog posts on the Internet. Simply conduct a search on Google.

Kerry Hook

Kerry Hook, the Frugal Retiree, has developed a very useful website (*thefrugalretiree.com*) for those of us in the retirement mode. You will find a variety of articles on how to live well for less covering such topics as money, humor, travel, medicine and more. She offers great advice on downsizing and meal preparation as well.

Recently she produced an article on how to make some additional income from the Internet as well as strategies for making money at home.

Arlene V. Poma

After a 23-year career with the State of California, Arlene was forced to retire. Writing is now her major passion. She resides in a 960-square-foot house in California.

Arlene offers some practical living tips for retirees taken from her personal experience.

- She suggests that if you stop buying fashionable clothes, you will save a substantial amount of money.
- In terms of personal upkeep, be sure to shop around for salon services.
- If you spend a fair amount of time at home, why not do your own housekeeping? The same applies to gardening, if you have gardening skills.
- Consider buying a smaller more economical vehicle, particularly if you are driving less. You may even be entitled to an auto insurance discount if you do not drive much.
- Hobbies are a major source of enjoyment for retirees. Choose your hobbies carefully and set a budget. Hobbies can be expensive. Allow yourself to grow slowly into your craft. Buy good used equipment for your hobby when you can. She also suggests that hobbies can easily turn into businesses. You may be able to sell your creations or teach classes.
- Poma believes that cash is king. If you are operating on a tight budget, try to pay for things with cash. This will obviously reduce credit card bills.

Betty Gerstein

According to a recent article in the AARP newspaper, Betty's entertainment budget, at age 80, is limited, so she has figured out how to take in shows, concerts, sporting events, the ballet, and even meals without putting out any money.

Her secret, which I've discussed previously, is to volunteer for just about everything.

In Florida, where she resides, she volunteers at an international tennis tournament where she sees great tennis and is fed. She also helps out at the local film festivals where she is able to see some great films.

In addition to all of the preceding, she volunteers at a community center that shows movies on Sunday mornings. During the summers she takes in concerts in the park that are free.

Mary and Richard Werling

This couple knew that during their retirement years they wanted affordable cultural events, access to free or low-cost college-level classes and in general, an active lifestyle.

When the couple relocated from a Washington D.C. suburb to a college town in Lexington, VA they were near two colleges. They can audit classes and attend student performances as well as other cultural events at the colleges.

The Werlings also enjoy visiting historic sites that are within driving distance to their new location.

Christina Gutt

One of the things that Christina Gutt does is to pick up the local newspaper for the purpose of examining the local community calendar.

She lost her job two years ago at the age of 64. She exists on her Social Security Benefit.

She has relocated out of New York City to Rochester, New York. She feels that Rochester has a rich cultural life, which includes large theaters as well as community venues for a fraction of the cost of Broadway shows. In addition, there is no shortage of city-sponsored events, particularly a variety of free festivals.

She also takes advantage of many activities offered at a nearby community center, such as weekly art classes, free lectures, and various day trips. Again, she is a big believer in checking out the local newspapers.

SUGGESTED READING

The Successful Retirement Guide, by Kevin Price (Rainbow Books, $19.95) offers suggestions on how to stay intellectually, socially, and physically engaged during retirement.

Retire Happy, by Richard Stim (Nolo Publishing, $19.99) presents suggestions for a happy retirement including some very useful planning tools.

How to Retire Overseas, by Kathleen Peddicord (Hudson Street Press, $25.95) discusses ideas for frugally relocating abroad.

How to Love Your Retirement, by Barbara Waxman (Hundreds of Books, LLC, $16.95) features narratives by hundreds of retirees who share their tips, tricks, and stories. Advice is also offered by expert contributors in the areas of finance, psychology, education, and health.

Retirementology, by Gregory Salisbury (FT Press, $23.99) offers retirement guidance regarding living, savings, and spending

Nextville, by Barbara Corcoran (Springboard Press, $24.99) suggests retirement locations and advice for relocation.

America's Cheapest Family, by Steve and Annette Economides (Three Rivers Press, $12.95) presents ideas for saving money.

The New Frugality, by Chris Farrell (Bloomsbury Press, $24) discusses ways to consume less, save more, and live better.

Reinventing Retirement, by Miriam Goodman (Chronicle Books, $24.95) suggests 389 bright ideas about family, friends, health, what to do, and where to live.

Reworking Retirement, by Allyn Freeman and Robert Gorman (Adams Media, $17.95) offers a practical guide for retirees returning to the workplace.

What Color is Your Parachute?, by John Nelson and Richard Bolles (Ten Speed Press, $19.99) helps you to plan for your dream retirement.

Living Large in Lean Times, by Clark Howard (Avery Press, $19) features 250 ways to buy smarter and save money, written by the host of the Clark Howard Show on CNN.

Retirement on a Budget, by John Howells (Globe Pequot Press, $15.95) discusses creative ways to save money in retirement.

Retiring Well on a Poor Man's Budget, by staff of AC&A (FC&A Publishing, $7.99) offers ways to stretch your retirement budget.

The AARP Retirement Survival Guide, by Julie Jason (Sterling Publishing, $14.95) discusses smart financial decisions in good times and bad.

The Cheapskate Next Door, by Jeff Yeager (Broadway Books, $12.99) presents specific frugal ways to live below your means in an effort to enjoy the good life.

The Money Class, by Suze Orman, (Spiegel & Grau, $26) offers suggestions to steer you and your family in the right direction financially.

The Couple's Retirement Puzzle, by Roberta Taylor, (Lincoln Street Press, $17.95) discusses ten important issues for consideration in the transition to retirement.

The Big Retirement Risk, by Erin Botsford, (Greenleaf Book Group Press, $21.95) presents new ways to think about retirement planning in an effort to create your own "preferred lifestyle" or "lifestyle driven planning."

Where to Retire, by John Howells, (Globe Pequot Press, $18.95) offers suggestions in regards to relocation. Howells makes specific recommendations about how to find your Shangri-la, and then goes on to discuss a variety of locations around the country.

Don't Buy Your Retirement Home Without Me, by Richard Andrews, (Wrightbooks, $29.95) presents specific advice on purchasing a home in a retirement community.

The Retirement Maze, by Rob Pascale, Louis Primavera, and Rip Roach, (Rowman & Littlefield, $36.00) helps retirees adjust to retirement and life outside the workforce.

WEBSITE DIRECTORY

Frugal Entertainment

bankrate.com – offers an extensive list of ways to entertain yourself

aarp.org – presents a variety of discounts on books, movies and games

hulu.com – offers free TV shows

redbox.com – online kiosk reservations

showuptickets.com – reduced prices on theatre tickets

apple.com/itunes – inexpensive movies and music

pandora.com – free access to radio stations

npr.com – download songs and concerts

restaurant.com – discount coupons to thousands of restaurants

spinner.com – downloads from 350 radio stations

jango.com – play music by selecting an artist

songstube.net – listen to music and watch videos for your favorite artists

billboard.com – top 100 songs listed

napster.com – (free Napster) the no cost companion to Napster

Frugal Senior Organizations and Websites

aarp.org – great frugal ideas for retirees

roadscholar.org (formerly Elderhostel) – learning adventures for people over the age of 55

seniorcorps.org – offers a variety of online courses to enhance senior's technology skills

americanseniors.org – information provided regarding ways to live healthier, wealthier lives

senior.org – represents interests and concerns of senior citizens

seniorshomeexchange.com – a frugal way to save money on

vacations through home exchanges
allthingsfrugal.com – frugal articles
frugal-retirement-living.com – offers a variety of frugal links
usa.gov – government sponsored site that features retirement links
moneyover55.about.com – information to help you take control of your spending habits
frugalliving.about.com – advice on how to improve your financial picture
retiredamericans.org – advice offered to protect and preserve programs relative to health and economic security
seniorresource.com – presents ways to reduce housing costs
babyboomers.org – offers deals on things that boomers need

Frugal Hobbies
traildino.com – database of hiking trails
railstotrails.org – hiking on former rail trails
trails.com – trail locator links
modernlibrary.com – suggestion offered reading novels and other literature
flickr.com – good source for posting and examining photos
photography.about.com – free course in photography
experiencecorps.org – a great source for volunteering
ancestry.com – presents data on ancestor's dates of birth
mygenealogysecrets.com – free mini-course on genealogy
basketmakers.com – baskets
autographcollector.com – autographs
comicbooks.about.com – comic art forms
fohbc.com – bottles
picassa.google.com – free online photo posting
flickr.com – free online photo posting
free-online-art-classes.com – courses offered in painting and drawing

ballroomdancers.com – free video dance lessons as well as music samples

Frugal Volunteering
serviceleader.org – virtual volunteering opportunities
volunteermatch.org - virtual volunteering assistance
elderwisdomcircle.org – virtual mentoring
seniorcorps.gov – RSVP offers a large amount volunteer resources
experiencecorps.org – pays stipends to tutor school children
crossculturalsolutions.org – international volunteer organization

Frugal Life Websites
frugalliving.about.com – offers many great suggestions
frugalvillage.net – ideas for frugal living
sustainablog.org
worldchanging.org
green.yahoo.com
freecycle.org
greendaily.com – eco-friendly suggestions
treehugger.com – sustainability ideas
greenmoneyjournal.com
slowfoodsusa.org
allthingsfrugal.com –articles that will save you money
frugal-retirement-living.com
retiredamericans.org – Alliance for Retired Americans
generationamerica.org
babyboomers.org
60plus.org
serviceleader.org – virtual volunteering can save money

Health

drugstore.com – discount prescription merchant

prescriptiongiant.com – see above

pharmnet.com – see above

EyeCareAmerica.org – free eye exams if you are over 65

aarp.org/food – frugal recipes and tips on food preparation from food experts

medtipster.com – pharmacy search engine for discounted generic drugs

ratemds.com – over a million free doctor reviews

discovertesting.com – testing information relating to a healthy home environment

caringinfo.org – initiative that promotes home healthcare towards the end of life

clinicaltrials.gov - a site which offers medical studies

claims.org – nonprofit dedicated to expert assistance for health claims issues

healthcarebluebook.com – free consumer guide that helps you determine fair prices in your area for healthcare services

Home

aarp.org/elderhousing – a good resource for cohousing resources

maccamant-durrett.com – examples of senior cohousing

delwebb.com – retirement communities around the country

nationalsharedhousing.org – lists of home sharing programs

seniorresource.com – shared housing resources

seniorhomesharing.org – promotes the creation of group homes where seniors live together as a family

homesharing.org – assists in locating a home share

homeaway.com – rental property listings

mhbay.com – mobile home park listings

usdirectory.com – more mobile home park listings

Personal Growth

ymca.net – a great place to find deals for senior citizens
   including trips and courses

uponline.com – University of Phoenix online allows you to
   work towards a college degree

yahoo.com/education – a great resource for distance education

free-ed.net – a collection of free courses in a variety of areas

word2word.com – links to free online courses in most languages

spanishromance.com – offers free resource to learn the Spanish
   language

learn-chinese-language-online.com – features information to
   help you to learn the Chinese language

learnoutloud.com – offers 3,000 free audio titles including
   books, lectures, and interviews

education-portal.com – lists free places to locate ebooks

seniornet.org – a frugal way to keep up with technology

itunes.com – all-inclusive source for various downloads

museumstuff.com – offers a large variety of educational links

coudal.com/moom.php – Museum of Online Museums

archives.icom.museum/vlmp/ - Virtual Library Museum Pages
   offers a directory of online museums

coudal.com/moon.php – museum links

archives.icom.museum/vlmp/ - worldwide directory of online
   museums

roadscholar.org – learning travel adventures

Relocation

findutopia.com – research locations to live and retire

ideal-places-to-retire.com – site offers detailed information on a
   variety of locations around the world

TopRetirements.com – offers a list of the ten worst states for
   retirement

aarp.com – ongoing articles regarding best places to retire *kiplinger.com* – site offers articles on relocation

Retirement Communities
delwebb.com – retirement communities around the country
retirenet.com – large network of retirement, independent living, assisted living, and community based retirement services with a search links.
55 communityguide.com – comprehensive directory of retirement communities and retirement homes
retirementcommunity.com – all-inclusive directory of retirement communities, retirement homes, and elder care facilities
55communityguide.com – active adult communities
retirementcommunitiesonline.com – national listings in Arizona, Florida, and more

Retirement Planning Tools
aarp.org/work/retirement-planning – a calculation system setup through a series of interviews
analyzenow.com – a one page worksheet that asks detailed questions with in converting future pension payments into current dollars
www3.trowprice.com/ric/ric/public.ric.do – T. Rowe Price income calculator with results that indicate projected monthly retirement income

Shopping
groupon.com – deal of the day site
dealchicken.com – another deal of the day site
buywithme.com
blackboardeats.com
yipit.com
gasbuddy.com
shopzilla.com – formerly Bizrate

pricegrabber.com – great deals on a variety of products
overstock.com – prices on excess merchandise
amazon.com – all purpose shopping including groceries
amazon.com/prime – special shipping arrangement for Amazon customers
walmart.com – grocery shopping available
smartsource.com – coupon clipping site
glassesunlimited.com – discount online eyeglass site
retailmenot.com – online coupon site
guru.com – online freelance marketplace
froogle.google.com – shopping search mechanism
shopping.com – shopping with price comparisons
dealchicken.com – deal of the day site
catalogs.com – catalog deals
crutchfield.com – high rated electronic shopping site
BHphotoVideo.com – high rated electronic shopping site
catalogs.com – discount offers
highpointfurniture.com – deals on American made furniture
buzzillions.com – product reviews
tigerdirect.com – electronic deals
newegg.com – more electronic deals
discounts.aarp.org – discounts galore offered to AARP members
gasbuddy.com – compares gas prices in your area

COUPONS
coupons.com – printable web coupons
restaurant.com - dine out for as much as 50% off
GeoQpons – a free app that allows you to use coupons right from your device
CouponMom.com – deals from supermarket chains
Groupon.com – big discounts in many cities

Travel

travelzoo.com – offers weekly emails relating to great travel deals

globalvolunteers.org – short-term volunteer vacations

volunteerabroadfree.com – opportunities to teach abroad

crossculturalsolutions.org – international volunteer vacations

elderhostel.org – over 55 learning adventures

intervac.com – house swapping listings in 50 countries

homeexchange.com – home exchange listings

resortime.com – time share rentals

condodirect.com – time share rentals

vrbo.com – vacation rentals by owners

aarp.org – great tips for frugal travelers

tripadvisor.com – impartial international travel reviews (I use this site regularly. It is fabulous.)

kayak.com – all inclusive travel search site

priceline.com – travel site with utilizing bidding process

seatguru.com – assistance with seat selection on airplanes

tripit.com – organizes your travel plans into one master itinerary

yapta.com – email alerts sent out when airfare prices drop

HopStop.com – travel directions via subway, bus, or taxi

lastminutetravel.com – great deals if you can wait

cruiseamerica.com – RV rental site

Additional great travel deal sites:
- *travelocity.com*
- *expedia.com*
- *orbitz.com*
- *costco.com*
- *hotwire.com*
- *kayak.com*
- *farecast.com*

- *farecompare.com*
- *airfarewatchdog.com*
- *fly.com*
- *carrentals.com*
- *cheaptickets.com*
- *cruise.com*
- *cruisecompete.com*
- *tripspot.com*
- *bookingbuddy.com*
- *aaa.com*
- *airgorilla.com*
- *betterbidding.com*
- *bestparking.com*
- *yapta.com*
- *rangeroamer.com*
- *quickbook.com*
- *megabus.com*

Volunteering

experiencecorps.org – literacy volunteering agency
seniorcorpsgov – Retired Seniors Volunteer Program
crossculturalsolutions.org – worldwide volunteering programs
experiencemattersaz.org – AZ based organization offering
    meaningful opportunities for experienced people
volunteermatch.org – community volunteering
americorps.gov – communities and nonprofits together
habitat.org – families and communities coming together
allforgood.org – sharing community volunteering activities
nps.gov – National Park Service volunteering
volunteer.gov – natural resource volunteer portal
proliteracy.org – advocates public policy
serviceleader.org – virtual volunteering

Volunteer Vacations
coloradotrail.org – programs for care of the Colorado Trail
wwoof.org – offers opportunities on organic farms
globalvolunteers.org – short term volunteer vacations on 6 continents
volunteerabroadfree.com – opportunities to teach abroad
flyforgood.com – an online trip finder that connects volunteers with nonprofits
travelocity.com/Travel For Good – partners with organizations that offers grants
outdoors.org – Appalachian Mountain Club
sierraclub.org – runs 80–90 volunteer vacations per year

Work Resources
seniorjobbank.com – online meeting place for over 50 job seekers beginning at entry level
seniors4hire.org – nationwide online career center for businesses that recruit and hire older workers
enrge.us – employed network for retired government workers
kforce.com – temporary work agency
kelleyservices.com – temporary work agency
manpower.com – temporary work agency
caretaker.org – listings for taking care of other people's property
retirementjobs.com – free employment service for seniors
workforce50.com – presents employment opportunities for people over 50
experienceworks.org – assists older workers in getting the training they need to find jobs
craigslist.org – offers job postings in more than 100 community sites in the U.S.
alpineaccess.com – virtual call center from home
arise.com – call answering service

careers.convergysworkathome.com – customer care agents

intellicare.com – call center

workingsolutions.com – home based customer service

2020research.com – market research service from home

ejury.com – online jury resource

onlineverdict.com – online jury resource

ivaa.org – virtual assistant resource

virtualassistantjobs.com – virtual assistant resource

careerbuilding.com – copyediting and proofreading job postings

cybereditor.com – writer and editor postings

tutor.com – online tutoring site

kaplankids.com – online tutoring site

idealist.org – information regarding working for nonprofit

encore.org – career reinvention information

bridgestar.org – nonprofit jobs

linkedin.com – professional employment opportunities and strategies

retiredbrains.com – employers looking for seasoned workers

grayhairmanagement.com – a resource for senior managers and executives to find work

aarp.org/work – links for working after retirement

comingofage.org – over 50 job resource site

CPSIA information can be obtained at www.ICGtesting.com
Printed in the USA
LVOW071509150213

320334LV00002B/197/P